PHILIP FARKAS

the art of BRASS playing

A treatise on the formation
and use of the brass player's
EMBOUCHURE

by Philip Farkas

Professor of Music, Indiana University. Solo hornist and horn in-
structor, Aspen Music Festival. Formerly solo hornist, Chicago
Symphony Orchestra, Boston Symphony Orchestra, Cleveland Or-
chestra, Kansas City Philharmonic. Formerly horn instructor,
Northwestern University, Cleveland Institute of Music, Kansas City
Conservatory, De Paul University, Roosevelt University.

Brass Publications,
Box 66,
Bloomington, Indiana

Copyright 1962 by Philip Farkas

Library of Congress Catalog Card Number 62-20149

Lithographed in U.S.A. by
EDWARDS BROTHERS, INC.
Ann Arbor, Michigan

Contents

1. The Embouchure's Function 5
    The Function of the Jaw
    The Mouthpiece Angle
    The Function of the Muscles
    Fine Points
    The Angle at Which the Lips are Held
    Lower Lip Discipline

2. Photographic Studies of Virtuoso Players 25

3. Mouthpiece Placement 32
    French Horn Mouthpiece Placement
    Trumpet and Cornet Mouthpiece Placement
    Trombone and Baritone Mouthpiece Place-
       ment
    Tuba Mouthpiece Placement
    Summary

4. Moist Versus Dry Lips 35

5. The Lip Aperture 38
    What Shape Lip Aperture?
    What Size Lip Aperture?
    Methods of Changing Lip Aperture Size

6. Articulation 45
    The Function of the Lips in Tonguing
    Clean, Firm Attack
    Sforzando Attack
    Legato Attack
    Staccato Tonguing
    Rapid Tonguing
    Double- and Triple-Tonguing
    Slurs and *Legato* Playing
    Vowel Sounds as an Aid to Slurring

7. Mouthpiece Pressure 53
    Common Pressure Problems
    Lateral Pressure

8. Breath Control 57
    Inhalation
    Exhalation
    Exhalation Resistance

9. Conclusion 65

Introduction

Philip Farkas was born in Chicago in 1914, and received his education in the public schools of that city. He had his first experience with a brass instrument when he studied the bugle for the cultural enhancement (?) of his Boy Scout troop. This led to two years' work with BB♭ Tuba in junior high school. When the transporting of this instrument was banned by the local public transportation authorities (namely, the streetcar conductor), he switched his allegiance to the French horn, not only because of its slightly more desirable portability, but also because of a certain immediate and deeply felt affinity for the horn. This feeling has remained all through the years, and the difficulties and challenges met in brass playing have only served to make his vocation as perennially stimulating as an absorbing hobby.

Following six years of horn study with Louis Dufrasne, the renowned horn player and teacher (1878-1941), Mr. Farkas joined the Chicago Civic Orchestra, the Chicago Symphony Orchestra's training school for aspiring symphony musicians. Three years of this training under the leadership of Eric Delamarter, the gifted assistant conductor of the Chicago Symphony Orchestra, led to the first horn chair in the newly organized Kansas City Philharmonic, conducted by Karl Krueger. Three years of this valuable experience enabled Mr. Farkas in 1937 to join the Chicago Symphony as first hornist under the direction of Frederick Stock. In 1941 Mr. Farkas became principal hornist in the Cleveland Orchestra, under the direction of Artur Rodzinski. In 1945 he accepted an invitation from Serge Koussevitzky to share the first chair position of the Boston Symphony with Willem Valkenier. When George Szell was appointed conductor of the Cleveland Orchestra, he brought Mr. Farkas back as his principal horn. With the appointment of Artur Rodzinski as conductor of the Chicago Symphony in 1947, Mr. Farkas came back to his home city as first horn, a position he held until 1960, at which time he resigned to become a professor of music at Indiana University, a position he holds at the time of this writing.

During the course of his career much time has been devoted to teaching and lecturing about the French horn, and Mr. Farkas has served as horn instructor at Kansas City Conservatory, Chicago Musical College, Cleveland Institute of Music, DePaul University, Roosevelt University, Northwestern University, the Aspen Festival and, of course, Indiana University.

Mr. Farkas states: "My qualifications as a brass teacher can in no way be based on an assumption that I, as a student, started out with a natural, perfectly formed embouchure. Quite to the contrary, I have had more than the usual share of embouchure troubles and misconceptions. The gradual solving of these problems has given me a far better insight into the correction of others' problems than if I had had a natural, but unanalyzed playing talent. Certain teaching experiences have given me an increased perception in solving various embouchure problems in others. As first-chair men in large symphonies are very likely to charge relatively high fees for lessons, there is a certain understandable financial reluctance on the part of students to study with these men, except as a last resort, when playing problems have become insurmountable. Therefore, these teachers get a disproportionately large number of students with unusual and seemingly hopeless problems. I have had my share of these, and although my earlier experience with these students was often discouraging, little by little a pattern began to appear, not only of embouchure problems and their apparently related causes, but of even more remote and subtle causes. Fortunately, at the same time, there seemed to appear the logical correction for each of these problems. After many years of teaching players with embouchure troubles, it would be difficult to imagine a type of problem that has not been met and solved several times as a result of this valuable experience.

Of my substantial number of former students who are now professional brass players, it is interesting to note that more often than not, these players succeeded *in spite of* the need to overcome some embouchure flaw. I would go so far as to state that the majority of today's fine professional brass players had serious enough embouchure difficulties as students that they were forced to learn to understand their playing needs far more thoroughly than their supposedly lucky colleagues who had "everything" from the first day they touched a mouthpiece to their lips. Whereas these "natural" players sooner or later flounder when some flaw insidiously creeps into their technique, the player who learned to correct his trouble as a student by careful analysis and practice can not only correct these problems as they occur but also can usually "nip them in the bud."

Therefore, barring actual physical malformation of the lips or teeth, I feel that it is perfectly possible and practical for the brass player to hope for and to expect a clear, well-defined solution to his particular embouchure problem or problems, and to that end this book is dedicated."

1. The Embouchure's Function

The word *embouchure* is derived from the French word, *bouche,* meaning mouth. The mouthpiece of a brass instrument is also referred to in French as an *embouchure*. However, we shall consider only the English usage of the word, as it pertains to the mouth. A good definition of the brass player's *embouchure* might be this: [The mouth, lip, chin and cheek muscles, tensed and shaped in a precise and cooperative manner, and then blown through for the purpose of setting the air-column into vibration when these lips are placed upon the mouthpiece of a brass instrument.] This sounds like a relatively simple definition and a condition which should not be difficult to achieve physically. But consider what this arrangement of various muscles must accomplish. First, they will have to vary their tension and conformation sufficiently to obtain a range of three or four octaves, approximately 36 to 48 different notes. Not only must these notes be well-in-tune, but they must also have good tone quality. Along with these basic requirements the embouchure is expected to have the flexibility to jump from one range of the instrument to the other lightly and quickly. But this is not all! The embouchure is required, in conjunction with the breath, to do all these things at various dynamic levels, ranging from an extremely soft *pianissimo* to a loud *fortissimo*. Consider that these relatively small muscles must accomplish all this with the strength and endurance to continue for several hours a day and you begin to gain new respect for what appeared at first to be a simple arrangement of muscles. Although the complete embouchure is complex, it is only a composite of many individually simple muscular functions, and when these are understood and applied, perhaps very gradually, one at a time, they can be assembled successfully into an excellent embouchure.

For the brass player the lips provide much the same function as the woodwind player's reed, being the source of vibration which is amplified and projected through the instrument. As the pitch of this vibration has a direct bearing on the pitch of the note produced, it may be readily understood that one of the embouchure's first requirements is the ability to change the pitch of its vibrations from the highest to the lowest notes inherent in the instrument. The vibration of the lips, of course, results from the breath being blown between them while they are being held in a state of tension. While it is the varying degrees of this tension which, to a large

extent, determines the pitch of the note, it is the function of the air-stream to vary the amount of volume from loud to soft. Later, however, we will see that these two functions are interrelated and must be used in conjunction with each other. We will also find that the tone quality is a direct result of the more or less successful combining of these two functions.

Another function of the lips which, strangely enough, is often overlooked by brass players, is our need to "attach" ourselves to the instrument so that the air-column is hermetically sealed or completely air-tight at the point of contact between lips and mouthpiece. In this respect the lips must act not only as the coupler, but must also become a sort of built-in "washer". Too often one can stand near a brass player while he is playing and become aware of the sizzling sound of escaping air which attests to the unsuccessful use of the embouchure for this purpose of sealing the lips to the instrument. Luckily, as we shall see later, when one uses the embouchure correctly in all its aspects, this problem of sealing the lips perfectly to the mouthpiece solves itself.

Now let us investigate the various means by which the lips, teeth, tongue, air-column, and even the mental attitude combine and cooperate to form the embouchure, truly an ingenious product of man's imagination.

When I was a youngster just starting to play the bugle, I became much intrigued during a visit to Chicago's wonderful Museum of Science and Industry by a contrivance there which was designed to demonstrate how the lips of a musician activate a cornet. I don't remember the details of the machine, but I recall opening valves and pulling levers and getting, as a result, several different pitched blats from the cornet. This led me to believe that perhaps one of the most constructive things a teacher could do for a brass student would be to give him an assortment of rubber tubing, an old piece of automobile inner-tube, a tank of compressed air, an old battered trumpet, and some tools. Then the student should be told to go ahead and invent or devise a contraption that would make the trumpet produce a tone. In the first place this would make the student think out what is required to produce a sound, and second, it would make him decide the order, angles, and general positioning of the various gadgets to be used, arming him with knowledge of what creates the vibration. How much better a start this would give him than the often used approach, "Put the horn up to your mouth and blow!"

Before starting your embouchure study, you should procure two pieces of essential equipment: a small mirror which can be placed on a music stand, held in one hand, or clamped in the instrument's lyre, which is then adjusted by bending gently until the embouchure is reflected as in Fig. 1, and a reasonable replica of a mouthpiece rim, perhaps on a little handle, and similar in feel to your own mouthpiece, as in Fig. 2. Several types are available for purchase. Such a rim is an absolute necessity to a brass player - student and teacher alike.

Following is a list of places where such a rim can be obtained:

Renold Schilke, Music Products, Inc., 223 West Lake St., Chicago, Illinois.
Vincent Bach, 50 South MacQuesten Parkway, Mount Vernon, N. Y.

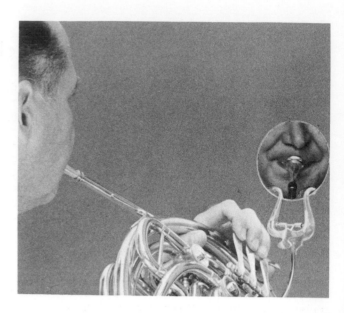

Fig. 1. Mirror held in lyre.

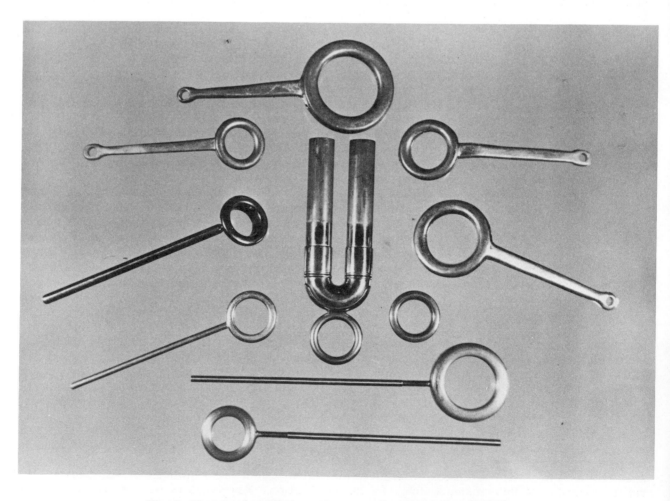

Fig. 2. Variety of mouthpiece rims, manufactured and makeshift.

Mr. H. E. Nutt, Vandercook College of Music, 3219 South Michigan Ave., Chicago, Illinois.
Brass Publications, P. O. Box 66, Bloomington, Indiana.

With a little manual skill a satisfactory rim can be made at home, perhaps by cutting the rim off an old mouthpiece with a hacksaw. In any case procure something, no matter how makeshift, which will approximate your mouthpiece rim and which can be held up to the lips for observation with the aid of the mirror.

The Function of the Jaw

Considering the embouchure as a mechanical contrivance, which in effect it is, we will discuss thoroughly each facet of its use.

One of the most important considerations is the direction and freedom of the air-stream. In designing our imaginary "horn-blowing machine", to bring the air from the compressed-air tank through gently curved tubing in the smoothest manner possible, direct it past some metal teeth, and continue it on between innertube rubber lips and then, just at the point where the air-stream enters the trumpet mouthpiece, violently deflect this air-stream downward at a sharp angle from its direction of a moment before, would simply go against all the dictates of logic. Yet I will venture a guess that fifty per cent of all embouchure problems are based directly on this illogical use of the air-column--this careful bringing up of a free air-column right from the "bottom of the lungs", letting it continue through an open, clear throat, and then, just where it would do some good as it enters the horn, violently deflect it with the lips so that it seeks to flow directly down over the chin and toward the floor.

By using the rim and mirror and feeling the air with your free hand, you can observe whether or not your air-column is continuing straight forward or is being deflected down your chin. When the air-column is found to deflect downward, in spite of the rim being held normally (that is, so the instrument, if it were attached, would point out more or less horizontally), it is almost invariably the fault of the lower jaw. We are concerned with having the upper and lower lips directly opposite each other, in an up and down consideration, so that they abut together, without one lip (usually the lower) sliding in behind the other. The foundation or support of the lips is the responsibility of the upper and lower front teeth. Therefore, if the lips are to line up so that they abut together without sliding one under the other, the upper and lower front teeth must also be exactly in line. As the upper jaw is immovable it becomes

the duty of the lower jaw to adjust this alignment of the teeth. Most of us find that the natural position of the lower jaw in repose is slightly receded so that the lower front teeth are behind the upper front teeth and the large flat surfaces of the back upper and lower molars are touching. We keep the jaw in this position so much of the time that we might be inclined to think of this as its "natural" position. However, there is another position of the lower jaw which we must consider equally natural, in spite of the fact that we do not use it quite so often. Nature gave us the ability to thrust out the lower jaw so that the upper and lower front teeth, or incisors, can meet in a snipping motion for the purpose of biting off pieces of food. Both these positions would be used, for instance, in eating a piece of celery. First the jaw would be thrust forward to enable the front teeth to bite off a piece of the celery. Then the jaw would be receded so that the upper and lower molars could reach each other for the purpose of masticating the celery.

I mention this simple example in order to emphasize the normality of *both* jaw positions, because so many brass players avoid this forward thrust of the jaw while playing, as though it were a most freakish and abnormal thing to do. The thrust-forward jaw position is not only normal, but, in my opinion, is an absolute necessity if one is to get that air-column directed straight through the horn for a big, rich and free tone. See Fig. 3.

To sum it up, I believe that the air-column must continue in a straight line through the mouth, the lips, and finally the horn. The only way this can be accomplished is by aligning the front teeth, and consequently the lips, by the proper amount of forward thrust of the lower jaw. This thrust must be used with judgment and sensitivity. Learn the degree of thrust needed by observing in the mirror and memorizing how the jaw feels when the upper and lower front teeth are exactly abutted together. When this is accomplished the teeth are then separated by lowering the jaw between one-eighth and one-quarter inch (the amount varying between individuals). Be careful not to let the jaw *recede* as it lowers. This forward jaw position should be very close to the theoretical ideal and should be changed very little, except as our various individual jaw and teeth formations (or malformations) dictate. To a player unaccustomed to this thrust of the jaw, the feeling at first might prove very disconcerting, but it is right and logical, and will soon feel normal if used carefully and conscientiously for a few days.

The Mouthpiece Angle

One additional change is usually necessary when

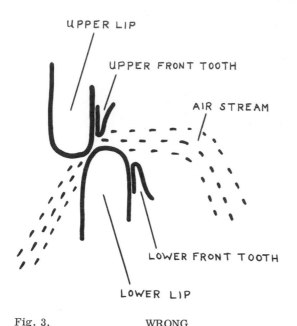

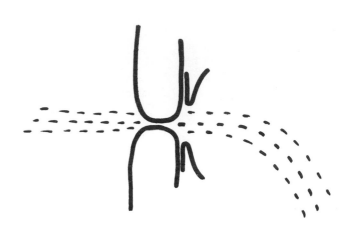

UPPER LIP

UPPER FRONT TOOTH

AIR STREAM

LOWER FRONT TOOTH

LOWER LIP

Fig. 3.   WRONG

Lower jaw receded. Lower front teeth not
as far forward as upper front teeth.

RIGHT

Lower jaw thrust forward to align lower
and upper front teeth.

this jaw thrust is first used. Most players who have unthinkingly learned to play with a receding lower jaw have also learned to compensate for this position by tilting the mouthpiece and instrument downward, to somewhat the same angle at which the clarinet is held. This is done instinctively to equalize the pressure on the upper and lower lips, which, of course, are not in good alignment because of the receding jaw. Therefore, when the jaw is thrust forward as recommended, *the angle of the instrument must be changed* so that the mouthpiece assumes a fairly horizontal position. The exact amount of this "horizontal improvement" must be carefully considered so that the mouthpiece pressure is *exactly* and *evenly* distributed on both lips.

When this jaw thrust and the change of mouthpiece angle to the correct position have been successfully accomplished, another serious flaw in many players will be painlessly and satisfyingly corrected. The receding jaw and downward pointed mouthpiece often cause the mouthpiece to "ride" or slide upward toward the player's nose, as mouthpiece pressure is applied in ascending passages. This is a most detrimental effect, rolling more and more upper lip and less and less lower lip into the mouthpiece as the player ascends in the instrument's range. Any brass player uses more pressure (no matter how small an amount) as he ascends in range, so it is almost impossible to avoid this effect as long

as the player continues to play with a downward angled mouthpiece and a receding jaw. Fig. 4 will help clarify the reason that this is so. From the diagram we can see that, in the picture labeled "wrong", the direction of the mouthpiece pressure is at an inclined angle to the flat and slippery surfaces of the front teeth and any increase or decrease in mouthpiece pressure (and this *does* take place, for us all!) is going to cause a sliding motion of the lips and mouthpiece against the front teeth. Common sense will point out the undesirable side effects brought on by this upsetting motion. Contrast this with the picture labeled "right". Here, no matter how much or how little pressure is used, and no matter how violently this pressure is varied, the fact that the mouthpiece pressure is exactly at right angles to the front teeth surfaces negates any desire the mouthpiece might have to "travel" either up or down.

So we find the angle of the mouthpiece to the lips is quite critical for *three* reasons. First, it must be aimed in the same direction that the air is traveling as it leaves the lips, or, considered from the more correct point of view, the lips must aim the air in the direction the mouthpiece is pointed. Second, the proper angle of mouthpiece to lips will distribute mouthpiece pressure evenly over both lips, which is vital to endurance and good tone. Third, when placed at right-angles to the teeth, and

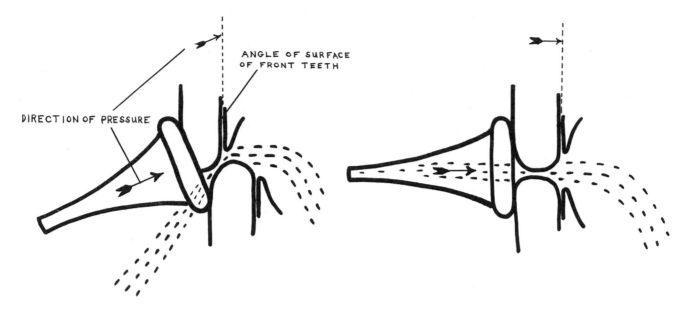

ANGLE OF SURFACE OF FRONT TEETH

DIRECTION OF PRESSURE

Fig. 4.   WRONG   RIGHT

1. Mouthpiece pressure unequal on upper & lower lip.
2. Air-stream deflects at downward angle to that of mouthpiece.
3. Mouthpiece pressure pushes back at oblique angle to tooth surfaces.

1. Mouthpiece pressure equal on upper & lower lip.
2. Air-stream aims directly into mouthpiece.
3. Mouthpiece pressure pushes back at perpendicular angle to tooth surfaces.

consequently to the lips, the mouthpiece will not tend to slide up or down during the playing of various registers.

Two observations might be helpful in determining the proper angle for the mouthpiece. 1.) Insist that the pressure be quite evenly distributed between the upper and lower lips. This is not too easy to determine for the player who has long been guilty of using greater pressure on one lip than the other, as one lip has been toughened and the other pampered by the unequal pressure. However, with care and judgment, in due time this pressure awareness will become very acute. After prolonged playing sessions observe the marks left on the lips by the mouthpiece. The varying severity of the marks on each lip can reveal much information as to which lip is bearing the brunt of the pressure. 2.) Play large intervals, perhaps octaves or even twelfths, in rather rapid succession, while noting in the mirror whether the mouthpiece wants to "ride" up on the lips when the mouthpiece pressure varies for these large intervals. If the mouthpiece seems to climb upward on the lips as the pressure (however mild) is applied for the upper note of the interval, it usually causes a very characteristic bulge of flesh between the mouthpiece and the nose. The chances are very great that the downward slant of the mouthpiece and

instrument is causing this push upward. The cure, of course, is to raise the angle of the instrument to a more horizontal position. In certain cases where this does not seem comfortable or practical, the same result can be obtained by tipping the head slightly more downward.

Although it occurs very rarely, I have met a few brass players whose jaw and teeth formation has influenced them to go to the opposite extreme and angle the mouthpiece much too high. The obvious correction of this fault is to recede the lower jaw somewhat and carefully equalize the lip pressure.

The foregoing discussion might lead one to believe that all players who play with a receding jaw tilt the instrument downward in an attempt to equalize the pressure on both lips. However, this is not the case. Occasionally we find one of these receding-jaw players who keeps the instrument at a normal horizontal angle. But his receding jaw directs the air downward so that it hits the bottom wall of the mouthpiece and at the same time puts all the pressure on the upper lip. Often, for such a player, a change in the angle of the horn and mouthpiece to the face is unnecessary. All this player need do is thrust the jaw forward the proper amount and the air will be blown straight ahead into the mouthpiece. In addition, the more forward position of the lower

10

lip will lift some of the mouthpiece pressure off the upper lip and distribute it equally.

As brass playing is not our Creator's primary reason for placing us upon this Earth, we are undoubtedly not ideally constructed for this art and must therefore learn to play in spite of our less-than-ideal physical adaptability. Perhaps this is the reason one can observe from the profile photographs of the brass players on pages 26 to 31 that the mouthpiece is not being held at a right angle to the players head, but points *slightly* down. This *slight* angle is not detrimental, as we probably all instinctively tend somewhat to this natural receding of the jaw. But what we must avoid is an *extreme* downward angle, one which could only take place when the jaw is definitely receded and one which permits the air-column to blow downward over the chin. Test for this with the rim.

Use a few simple exercises to learn what the jaw and lip positions can accomplish in directing that all-important air-column. Try to blow air, without benefit of rim or mouthpiece, directly downward, so that it can be felt flowing past the chin. In order to achieve this, one must recede the lower jaw in an extreme manner, at the same time pulling the lower lip in and under the upper. Now try to blow the air in the opposite direction, so that it actually blows up toward the nose and into the nostrils. In accomplishing this act, one almost instinctively thrusts out the lower jaw to a bulldog-like position, pouts out the lower lip, and at the same time pulls the upper lip in and behind the lower. Although both these air-directing exercises are extreme, they will demonstrate that the jaw and lips are the influencing factors in pointing the air into (or *not* into!) the mouthpiece. They will also demonstrate the tremendous change in angle that the air-column is capable of undergoing as it leaves the lips--almost 180°!

The third and most important exercise consists of using the jaw and lips to modify the results of the first two exercises, so that the air blows *directly* forward, in the same direction that the mouthpiece would point, were it being held in correct playing position. The direction of the air current can be very accurately determined by using the hand and observing in the mirror. Hold the hand up and feel for the air current. Better yet, move a thin little strip of tissue paper edgewise in the vicinity of the air-stream until it flutters. When the air-stream is really under control and can be directed *forward* with assurance, one can assume that the resulting jaw and lip position are very close to the best and proper setting. Next the mouthpiece rim should be placed on the lips to determine whether or not its added influence will disturb the air-column's forward direction. If the pressure of the rim is proper-

ly balanced between upper and lower lips, the air should continue straight ahead. The angle which the rim assumes in order to obtain this even pressure and the "straight ahead" direction of the air will furnish another valuable clue as to the proper mouthpiece angle to the player's face.

The Function of the Muscles

Thus far we have mainly considered the hard structure--the skeletal foundation of the embouchure--consisting of the jawbone and the teeth. We have investigated the various positions that these components can assume and it is now time to discuss the muscular structure which covers this foundation.

We know that in order to produce a sound on a brass instrument we must vibrate the lips into the mouthpiece by means of the air-stream. In order to create this vibration, certain muscles of the embouchure must be tensed. We all realize that the vibration set up in *any* musical instrument is dependent on an inherent tension somewhere in the sound source, be it the taut head on a drum, the tightly tuned string on a stringed instrument, the springy reed of a woodwind, or the tensed vocal cords of the singer. In comparing the embouchure to any of these, we must choose the vocal cords as the most apt analogy. Our lips, like our vocal cords, are part of us—muscle and flesh. Both are tensed or relaxed voluntarily at command of the brain and both are activated by the air column passing between them. No wonder brass teachers are always exhorting their pupils to "sing". As a matter of fact, we brass players actually do sing--substituting the lips for the vocal cords and using the instrument as a sort of glorified amplifier. When the muscles involved are used correctly, this singing or vibrating of the lips will enable the player to cover three or more octaves on the instrument.

Before considering this muscular action in detail, we should remember that a muscle, any muscle, can do just one positive thing—*it can contract*. When it does this, it grows shorter from end to end. Thus any member of the body to which the end of this muscle is attached will be pulled upon during the contraction of the muscle. As the muscle gets shorter upon contraction, it must necessarily get thicker at the same time. A muscle can do one more thing, but in a negative manner—it can relax. It is the interplay of these various muscle combinations contracting and relaxing that enable us to accomplish any physical movement, such as walking or lifting an arm. Let us examine the mechanics of a simple, everyday (I hope!) action closely related to brass playing—smiling. Most people unthinkingly assume that the mouth does the smiling. But does it? When we smile, the *cheek muscles* contract, and being attached to the corners of the mouth, exert an outward pull as they are shortened. Simultaneously, the lip and mouth muscles must cooperate by *relaxing* so that the cheeks can stretch them unresistingly into a smile. So while we are smiling, the contracted cheek muscles are thicker than usual, while the lips are stretched thinner than usual. At this time, these thinly stretched lips, being necessarily relaxed, are very vulnerable to injury (perhaps from a tightly pressed mouthpiece!). Possibly some readers who use a "smiling embouchure" are

already beginning to get a clue to their many embouchure woes from the few remarks above.

Perhaps a description of the *general* function of all the muscles which co-ordinate in forming the embouchure will give us the best foundation for later detailed discussion. As we did earlier, let us in imagination construct another contrivance, which will duplicate the embouchure's function. See Figs. 5, 6, 7 and 8.

We shall start with an empty coffee can, without a lid. Crude as the analogy may seem, because it is a hard shell, this coffee can will represent the

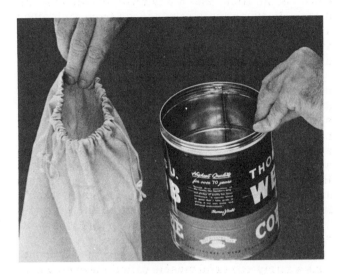

Fig. 5. Coffee can and cloth bag.

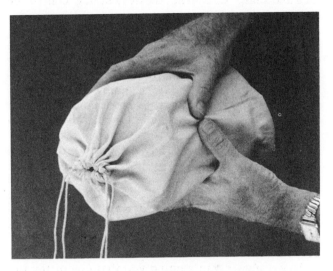

Fig. 6. Coffee can inside bag, drawstring tight - bag loose.

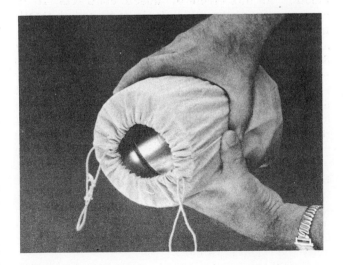

Fig. 7. Coffee can inside bag, drawstring loose—bag tight.

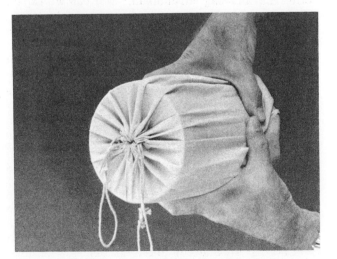

Fig. 8. Coffee can inside bag, drawstring tight - bag tight, forming vibrant tympanum or "drumhead."

brass player's skull (certainly not because it is hollow!). Next we procure a cloth bag, similar to the marble-bag of our childhood. This must be soft and flexible, similar in shape to the coffee can, and somewhat larger. The open end must have a hem with a drawstring run through it in such a manner that when the two ends of this string are pulled, the opening in the bag is drawn shut in a puckered manner, so that only a tiny circular opening--less than an eighth of an inch in diameter--remains. The coffee can is placed in this bag so that the open end is facing the same direction as the open end of the bag. The bag will now represent the entire covering of the skull, including muscles, flesh and skin of the face and scalp. Of course, the drawstring-controlled opening in the bag is going to represent the player's mouth. We now have this situation: a hard, inflexible shell which cannot change size or shape (the coffee can "skull"), surrounded by a strong, but very flexible covering (the cloth bag "facial mask"). This covering is capable of being drawn *fairly* smooth over the hard shell by the simple expedient of pulling the drawstring and closing the opening. However, as the bag, you remember, is slightly larger than the coffee can, it cannot be made to stretch tightly because, even when tightly closed, the bag's dimensions are slightly too large to achieve this. Thus we will have a sort of loose, baggy diaphragm over the open end of the coffee can--an untightened drumhead, if you please--with a little hole in the center, created by the tight drawstring. See Fig. 6.

Now I must again remind you that one of the important conditions of a musical vibration is *tension*. We would not expect a real drumhead to vibrate when struck, if it were as loose and flabby as our coffee can-and-bag "drumhead." Nor can we expect this home-made drumhead, our "mechanical embouchure", to vibrate. In many ways the brass player's embouchure resembles a taut diaphragm, like the drumhead, except that it is motivated, not by striking, but by a long thread of air rubbing against a tiny opening in its center. Neither can we expect this tympanum to vibrate with conditions reversed. If the drawstring is left in a loose condition while the bag is drawn tight over the coffee can, we have a different, but equally ridiculous condition, which will be just as unsuccessful as a vibrating medium. See Fig. 7.

In order to put our little coffee can drumhead into vibratory condition, we must do two simple things. First, we must gather a fistfull of the slack cloth at the bottom and sides of the bag and pull it tight so that all slack is taken up. Second, we must pull the drawstring tight. See Fig. 8. *Then* the little drumhead over the top of the can will be sufficiently

tight that it will vibrate if tapped with the finger tip, or more to the point, if a stream of air is sent forcibly through the little puckered opening. Note carefully that it takes *two* acts to achieve this vibratory condition: the drawstring opening has to be pulled almost completely closed, and the slack in the bag must be gathered up. If either the opening is left loose, or the bag left slack, the tension necessary for vibration will not occur. We might even compose a simple formula from these facts: For most musical vibrations to take place, the needed tension is obtained by forces which pull in opposite directions--a sort of tug-of-war. This is why piano and violin strings have to be secured tightly at *both* ends. Some time, watch a tympani player tune his drums. He tunes the screws across from each other as though they worked in pairs, because he is fully aware that the needed tensions for a good vibration are diametrically opposed to each other.

Now let us examine the similarities of the brass player's embouchure to these various mechanical devices we have constructed in imagination. The skull, jawbone and teeth are made, like the coffee can, of inflexible material, and cannot be altered to any degree, so that we will have to make do with whatever Nature has endowed us in that respect. However, the facial mask, including cheeks, chin and lips, are all, like the cloth bag, remarkably flexible, and over these components we have almost complete voluntary command as to what they will do and when they will do it.

Around the entire circumference of the mouth runs a fairly powerful muscle called the *orbicularis oris*. See Fig. 9. This muscle, like all others, has the ability to *contract*. Being practically circular, it contracts around the entire perimeter of the mouth. As this circle of muscle contracts, it, of course, makes a smaller circle of the mouth itself. In this way, it acts almost exactly like the drawstring in the bag. This lip contraction is perfectly demonstrated when one whistles (or cools tomato soup!). However, in brass playing such an embouchure is not completely successful. It is correct as far as it goes, but you remember that our coffee can drumhead was not successful either, with only the drawstring pulled tight. But when we tightened up the cloth at the back of the bag with the fist, we obtained the necessary tension to create vibration. Naturally, we cannot reach around and gather our loose skin and flesh to the back of the head. Nevertheless there is something that we can do which is equally effective and much more comfortable. We can *contract* certain muscles of the face and get exactly the tension we need.

The cheeks have large, strong muscles. See Fig. 9. When these contract they pull at the corners of the mouth and attempt to stretch it into a smile. The chin also has powerful muscles which are interwoven in a rather complex manner. See Fig. 9. This enables the chin to move in many directions. Of all these directions the chin can, and should contract with a downward pull, which will tend to pull the lower lip down. Altogether there are twenty-two or more of these muscles radiating out from the center of the mouth. A good way to observe them all working at once while the *orbicularis oris* relaxes is to simply yawn.

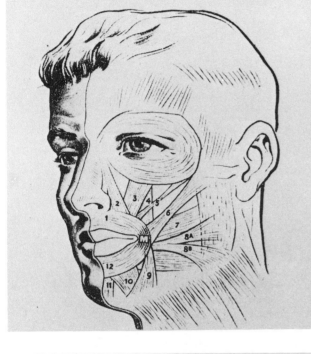

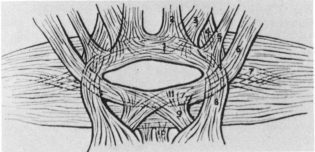

Fig. 9. M, modiolus. 1, orbicularis oris (upper lip portion). 2, levator labii sup. alaeque nasi. 3, levator labii superioris. 4, levator anguli oris. 5, zygomaticus minor. 6, zygomaticus major. 7, buccinator. 8a, risorius (masseteric strand). 8b, risorius (platysma strand). 9, depressor anguli oris. 10, depressor labii inferioris. 11, mentalis. 12, orbicularis oris (lower lip portion).

Reprinted with the permission of the publisher from BRASS TODAY edited by Frank Wright. Published 1957 by Besson and Company, Ltd., London.

Then there is the jaw itself. Along with its ability to thrust forward, it can also pull down, separating the upper and lower teeth to any desired distance. This lowering of the jaw also strives to stretch the mouth open in a vertical direction.

So we see that there are several forces at work in forming the embouchure. The drawstring of muscle around the mouth contracts in an attempt to form a very small circle of the mouth, but at the same time the cheek, chin and jaw muscles, in fact the complete network of muscles radiating out from the mouth, are striving to pull the mouth wide open in all directions.

Although these opposing muscles seem to be working at cross purposes, it is exactly this stress or tug-of-war which is needed to supply the tension so necessary to the creation of lip vibration. This tug-of-war is not violent, however. The tension is quite noticeable (though not painfully so!) in the highest register and gradually decreases in intensity toward the low register, until, for the very lowest notes, it seems almost non-existent. Nevertheless, it must still be there, even though the opposing muscles might figuratively say to each other, "You pull less hard and I will, too, but let neither of us win this tug-of-war."

Perhaps the above discussion will make us realize the futility of the age-old argument among brass players: "Which is the proper embouchure, the smiling one or the puckered one?" A little thought will lead to the conclusion that both systems *must be combined.* To argue otherwise would be as ridiculous as discussing which is the more important end of a violin string to fasten to the instrument, the end which is attached to the tuning peg or the end which is attached to the tail-piece. Although both points of view might be half right, they will also be half wrong. *Both* ends of the string, of course, must be firmly attached, or there will be no vibration. Similarly, all the "out-pulling" muscles of the face must contract at the same time that the ring of "ingathering" muscles around the mouth contracts, or we do not have our diametrically opposed tensions. If the lips are puckered, no matter how intensely, but the cheek and chin muscles remain flaccid, the lips will remain soft and without the resilience so necessary in producing a clear, ringing tone. Conversely, if the cheek and chin muscles contract vigorously, but the mouth-encircling muscle remains relaxed, the lips will be *pulled* into a wide smile which conceivably might, because of its stretched condition, have enough resilience to create a vibration. But at what expense to endurance and tone! The tone will be hard, bright and thin. Endurance, however, is the phase of playing which suffers most. The poor, thin-stretched lips are

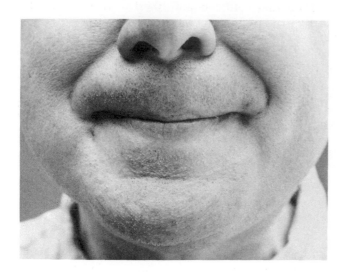

Fig. 10. Lips stretched into broad smile. Incorrect.

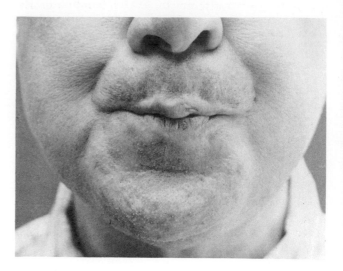

Fig. 11. Lips puckered in an extreme manner. Incorrect.

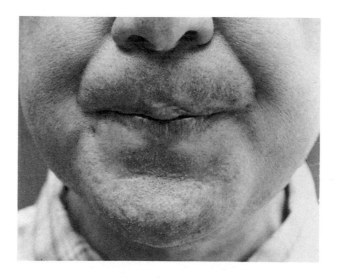

Fig. 12. Smile and pucker balance each other, resulting in puckered smile. Correct.

absolutely defenseless against pressure, as they must necessarily be in a relaxed condition in order for the cheek muscles to stretch them. Even a moderately light mouthpiece pressure can, in due time, punish such lips into insensibility. All our natural instincts require any muscle to contract when injury or punishment seems imminent. When suddenly expecting a punch in the stomach, any of us will involuntarily contract the abdominal muscles. This is Nature's way of protecting us from serious injury. Perhaps if we would consider the mouthpiece pressure applied during an entire day's playing time as a kind of long-drawn-out punch or blow on the lips, we would realize the need of constantly warding off this blow with the protection afforded by contracted lip muscles. *Fortunately for all brass players, this act of contracting the mouth muscles, in defense against mouthpiece pressure and the general fatigue of playing, is exactly the same action which puts the lips in perfect condition, when combined with the contracting of cheek and chin muscles, to produce the correct embouchure—from a vibration standpoint. So we find this contraction of the mouth muscles essential for at least two reasons: endurance and good vibration.*

We have discussed the *general* function of the facial muscles in forming the embouchure. Now it would be proper to discuss each of these muscles individually and in greater detail. The cheek muscles, because their function is so often misunderstood, will be considered first. See Fig. 9. These muscles are very strong and highly developed, perhaps because they are used so continually for talking and for facial expressions. Because of this strong development and familiarity of use, the beginning brass player almost automatically tends to draw the corners of the mouth into a broad smile by a strong contraction of the cheek muscles. See Fig. 10. Sooner or later he is told that this is wrong and that he must not smile. He then goes to the other extreme and learns to pucker his lips. See Fig. 11. But in order to facilitate this act, he relaxes the cheeks. Now he gets equally bad results, but for a different reason. The correct way to help this student, I believe, is to encourage the use of the cheek muscles, but insist that an equal amount of effort be used to contract the lip muscles, so as to "fight" the attempt to smile. Here are several exercises, devised to individualize and clarify the various muscular controls. While doing these, be sure to observe the action in the mirror. Start by forming a broad smile, very consciously contracting the cheek muscles, at the same time completely relaxing the lips so they can be stretched quite thin. Then slowly start puckering or contracting the lip muscles, pulling the mouth corners closer together, but, at the same time, very carefully keep the cheek muscles "locked" in their contracted condition. Perform this exercise, alternating with a moment of complete relaxation, every five or six seconds for a couple of minutes a day. This will not only educate the cheek and lip muscles, but will also develop their strength. During the exercise, watch for the point at which the contracting lip muscles have pulled the mouth into a sort of puckered smile, one in which the mouth is just a slight bit shorter from corner to corner than it would be in repose. See Fig. 12.

We are trying, in this exercise, to locate that perfect balance-point between the cheek and lip muscles, where neither the smile nor the pucker wins the tug-of-war. When this is found, the entire range of the instrument can be encompassed with almost no apparent change in the distance between the corners of the mouth. In other words, the mouth corners do not move for ascending or descending passages. However, the feeling of changing tension in the corners of the mouth is quite distinct. As we go higher in range, the tension of the contracting muscles mounts, but so evenly between cheeks and lips that the mouth corners have no tendency to move in either direction. Both teams in our tug-of-war increase their strength, but in exactly the same proportion, so that neither team comes any closer to winning than it did when both teams were weaker (in the lower register). It is understandable why this method of progressing up or down the range of the instrument can be accomplished with so little lip commotion. The cheek and lip muscles, and consequently the mouth corners, do not move, even though they might try, because their contractions *exactly* offset each other. So the muscular feeling while playing throughout the instrument's range is one of varying degrees of tension and relaxation *but not one of lip motion*—or commotion.

A second exercise will be found helpful in developing this feeling of tension-balance between cheek and lip muscles. It is exactly the opposite of the first exercise and is started by forming a strong contraction of the ring of muscle surrounding the mouth. While this is being done, be sure to keep the cheek muscles completely relaxed. This contraction will closely resemble the lip position while one attempts to whistle a very high note. Note that the similarity applies also to the cheeks, which should remain relaxed as when whistling. Then, while keeping the lips contracted, start to slowly contract the cheek muscles, as in smiling. As with the first exercise, do this one for several minutes a day, about ten times a minute, with a few seconds rest between each cycle. Remember that the two objectives are: 1.) to develop the sense of balance between the two opposing forces so that the lips are in a half-smiling, half-puckered condition, and 2.) to develop the muscular strength to maintain this balanced-tension over a fairly long period of time, such as would be encountered during the playing of a long musical passage. It is interesting to note that a *good* brass player, using this combination of puckered-smile, when he finally must stop because of fatigue (and this should not occur for several playing hours), does so because the *corners of the mouth* give way. Mouthpiece pressure is *never* the reason for such a player stopping. The puckered mouth is adequate protection against whatever mouthpiece pressure is needed. The corners of the mouth, being the focal point, or more graphically, the "center mark" of our imaginary tug-of-war rope, will fatigue

16

long before mouthpiece pressure causes cessation of playing. Therefore, a very good test of one's correct use of the embouchure is a careful observation of which muscles first feel fatigued. When the mouth corners tire, new users of this embouchure often become disheartened, feeling that something is wrong. Contrarily, they should feel encouraged, as this is the correct place to feel fatigue. Patience and practice will extend the playing time remarkably before this fatigue sets in.

The player who *should* worry is the one who feels his first fatigue at the point where the lips touch the mouthpiece. He is using too much pressure, or lips stretched thin, or, more usually, *both*. When such a player, in desperation, finally learns to play on contracted lips, this pressure can no longer cause so much harm, even though he, at first, cannot find the confidence to actually lighten the pressure. After a time he will begin to trust the ability of the puckered lips to obtain high notes by their own inherent tension, and he can, as the lip muscles strengthen, alleviate pressure little by little.

During many years of observation, I have never met a player who could honestly say that he always used a particular amount of mouthpiece pressure. As we become tired (and we all do when the concert is long enough, the notes loud enough, and the range high enough!), we tend to use more and more pressure. Thus we apply variable amounts of pressure, depending on our state of fatigue and the altitude and volume of the passage being played. This is pointed out to warn against believing too wholeheartedly the claims of some who profess never to use any pressure whatever. If one will use the strength inherent in the puckered-smile type of embouchure, he can eliminate a great deal of pressure. For not until it tires, must he resort to more pressure. Therefore, even the most correct player, as his embouchure slowly fatigues, must slowly but surely increase mouthpiece pressure. However, in this last statement lies a great ray of hope for the player who seems destined always to need too much mouthpiece pressure, because the corollary statement is equally true. If such a player will slowly and steadily build up the muscles that, by contraction, correctly tension the embouchure, he can just as gradually and steadily eliminate the need for excessive mouthpiece pressure.

In this discussion of the muscles which make up the embouchure, there still remains a group which must be given most careful consideration because of its importance. This is the rather complex group of muscles which comprise the chin. The interweaving of these muscles enables the chin, by their various combinations of contraction and relaxation, to pull upward toward the mouth, or downward and

outward. See Fig. 9. This remarkable versatility of the chin is most important to good brass playing, but unfortunately this same versatility makes it all too easy to use the chin in an entirely wrong manner. I feel certain that, next to the improper "wide-smile" embouchure, the most common playing fault is the incorrect use of the chin. This fault usually consists of a pronounced upward thrust of the chin, so that a "button" chin is formed. Characteristic of this upward-bunched position is the remarkable similarity in appearance of the chin to a peach-stone. The chin then looks like a large oval-shaped button and has numerous little "dimples" in it, very reminiscent of the pits in a peach-stone. See Fig. 13. These dimples are the tendon ends of many little muscles which are pulling the chin up, and their presence can be accepted as a sure indication that the chin is being tensed in exactly the wrong direction. Another characteristic sign one must be aware of is a small, deep, horizontal wrinkle which appears about half an inch below the lower lip when the chin is bunched up incorrectly. See Fig. 13.

When the chin muscles are functioning correctly, the chin distinctly arches downward and outward, and this little wrinkle is stretched completely out of existence. There is visual evidence of large muscles pulling the chin downward: one in the center pulling vertically downward to the tip of the chin, and one on each side of the chin, starting in the vicinity of each corner of the mouth and running diagonally downward and inward toward the center of the chin tip. See Fig. 14. When all these muscles are functioning correctly, they form a wide "U" shaped valley, the base of which is located just above the tip of the chin, and the sides of which run up into the corners of the mouth. See Fig. 14. This characteristic appearance is usually very apparent in any good brass player (observe it in the pages of players' photographs), and must be emphatically sought by the brass student.

Two beneficial exercises are suggested for the development of these muscles and for putting them to proper use. The first consists of simply "waking up" all the various chin muscles by moving them in every conceivable direction. Form the chin upward into a hard knot, then stretch it downward into the longest chin possible. Try to widen it by contracting the muscles on each side. Then try to put the chin over to one side by tightening the muscles on that side while relaxing those on the other. A little practice will "awaken" and strengthen muscles long unused. Bear in mind that some of these chin formations are undesirable, while others are exactly what we have been seeking.

When the chin can be controlled perfectly and moved in any direction at will, start to emphasize

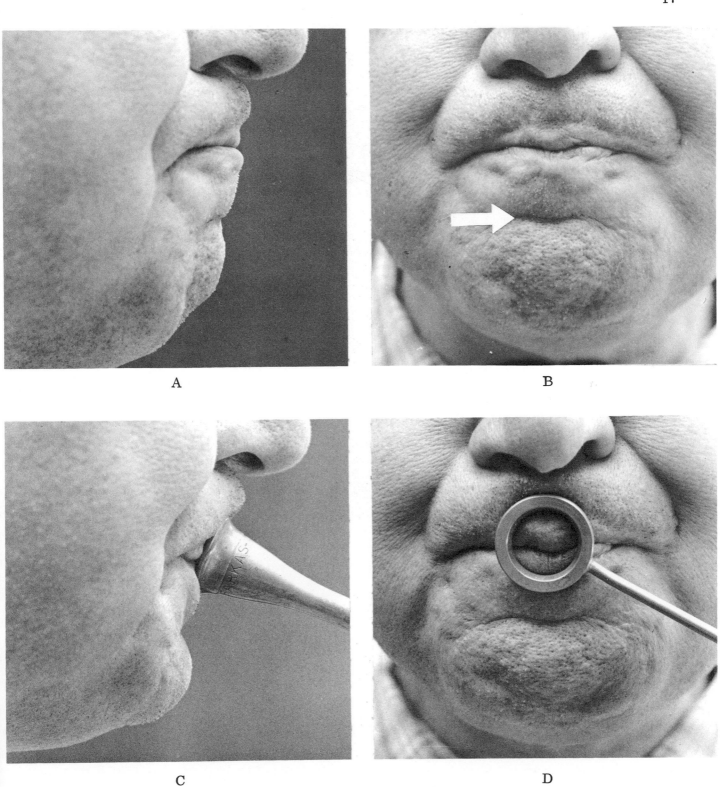

A

B

C

D

Fig. 13. Illustration A shows profile view of chin "bunched-up" incorrectly. Illustration B shows resemblance of "bunched-up" chin to peach stone. Incorrect. Arrow points to characteristic wrinkle, which should be avoided. Illustration C shows profile while playing. Horizontal wrinkle not sufficiently stretched out of existence. Illustration D shows how "bunched-up" chin chokes up lip aperture, adversely affecting the tone.

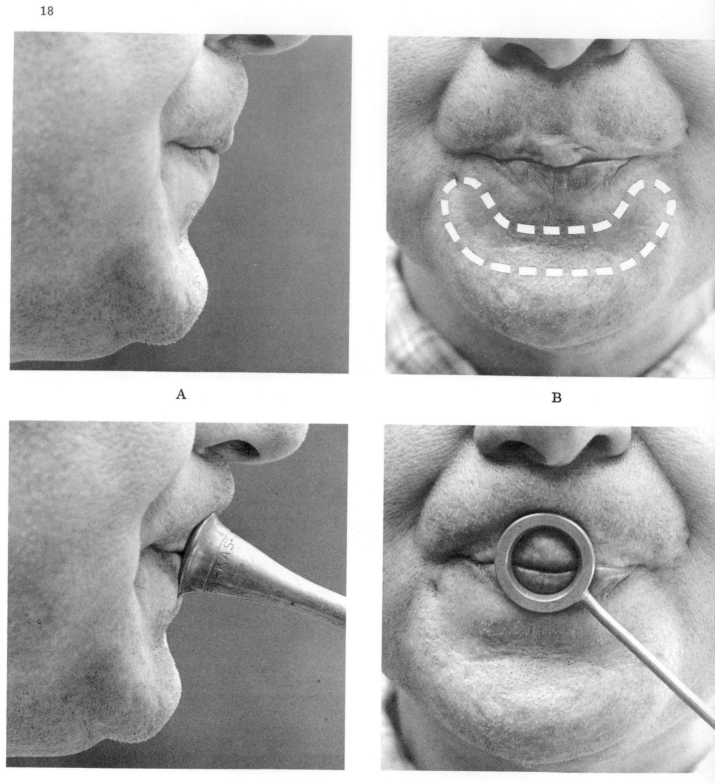

A

B

C

D

Fig. 14. Illustration A shows profile view of chin arched down correctly. Illustration B shows how horizontal wrinkle must be stretched out of existence. Dotted line outlines typical "U" shaped valley found so often in good players. Illustration C shows correct arching of chin, with no evidence of horizontal wrinkle. Illustration D shows how properly arched-down chin smooths flesh inside mouthpiece, allowing free vibration of edges of aperture.

the downward pull which causes that characteristic "U" shaped indentation to appear.

A second beneficial exercise consists simply of buzzing the lips without applying the mouthpiece or rim. Be careful to keep the lips opposite one another so that one (usually the lower) is not "swallowed" behind the other. It is almost impossible to get a good resounding buzz without pulling the chin down firmly in exactly the correct manner. For most brass players a middle "C", concert pitch, is a good, clear and practical note to intone in the first attempts.

Without the mouthpiece to restrict observation, it is possible to see the effect on the lower lip of this arching and pulling down of the chin. Notice how the lower lip, in its need to be tensed and arched open, is aided by this pull of the chin. While continuing to buzz the lips, carefully and delicately bring the mouthpiece and horn into playing position, and try to maintain the embouchure so that no change takes place at the moment the mouthpiece touches the lips. All too often the player used to a faulty chin position will revert back to his old habit the very instant the mouthpiece is felt. This is simply a reflex action based on a well-established bad habit and can be corrected with patience and perseverance. When finally accomplished, the chin will easily assume the same arched-down position achieved during unaided buzzing, even when the mouthpiece is in playing position. This chin position is so essential to correct playing that I feel perfectly safe in stating that no great advance can be made by a brass player until he has completely conquered this problem. It might help to emphasize this fact if the student will observe the best brass men in action, watching specifically for the arched-down chin. This can be done while playing with groups which contain good players. Or take a pair of binoculars to a symphony concert. Often fine brass players are shown very close-up on television. Music magazines usually contain excellent photos of well-known players in action. It might even be constructive to clip such pictures for assembly in a scrapbook. And, of course, restudy the pictures of the fine players in this book. To an observant student, close, intelligent scrutiny during these various contacts with fine players (need I say, *ignore* the bad ones!) can constitute an excellent aid to learning.

When the student has observed many top players for a while, he becomes distinctly aware that there exists a very definite facial expression while a fine brass player is performing (regardless of which instrument he plays), which could be referred to as *"the brass player's face"*. This facial expression is a composite of several different individual muscle positions, but the complete expression is very

characteristic, and an experienced player could spot a fraud immediately, while glancing through a group of photographs of fine professional players. Here are some of the features which are evident in the face of a good brass player while he is playing his instrument (observe these features in the pages of players' photographs). His jaw will be thrust out moderately, giving even the most chinless player a rather aggressive look. The cheeks will be taut as when one smiles, with perhaps a "parenthesis mark" around the corner of each side of the mouth. Yet when we study the mouth itself, we see that, in spite of the smiling appearance of the cheeks, the mouth is slightly puckered and not stretched into a smile. The chin will be pulled down and the muscles at either side will be quite prominent, resulting in that "U" shaped concavity whose base is just above the point of the chin. There is an indication, although sometimes hard to define, that the jaw, beside having a forward thrust, is being held open so that there is good clearance between the upper and lower front teeth.

These features of the embouchure may be observed one-by-one, and yet, when they are combined, they total that unmistakable "brass player's face", with its look of strength and determination.

The actor learns to portray an expression of pleasure, surprise, determination, etc., by first studying the individual movements required by the mouth, chin, eyebrows, etc., and then combining them to create the overall effect. When this is thoroughly learned he has only to think of the expression desired, and each part of the entire complicated facial structure immediately assumes its correct position, and the expression is formed. I believe that the training we, as brass players, require is very similar to this. We must learn the functions of each muscle in the face individually. Then we co-ordinate several of these functions at the same time. Finally we co-ordinate all of them and form a correct embouchure. But the time soon arrives, after this complete co-ordination has been rehearsed often enough, that we think of the cooperation of these muscles as creating a facial expression. From this time on we can bring into play all the needed components for a fine embouchure--not by laboriously recalling them one by one--but by instantaneously forming *the expression*, "the brass player's face".

Embouchure Fine Points

One of the most discouraging aspects of brass playing is the fact that the slightest deviation from the correct method can cause complete chaos in the functioning of the embouchure. We have considered the major requirements of the embouchure at some length and we should now discuss the minor elements one at a time. Perhaps *minor elements* is a misleading phrase, as some of them, incorrectly used, can cause as much havoc as a major flaw. I think of them as minor only because they can usually be more easily corrected than some of our larger problems. Perhaps they are minor, too, because they are so physically small as to sometimes defy detection. This is perhaps the most devilish thing about them. The study of the embouchure in the mirror—even to the extent of using a magnifying glass—sometimes does not seem to help. We instinctively know when something is wrong with our playing, although everything might appear correct and normal. It doesn't sound right, it doesn't feel comfortable, or perhaps we tire too quickly. There are a multitude of little clues when something is wrong, and yet we cannot quite decipher what it is that causes the poor results. The eye cannot detect the trouble, perhaps because it is so microscopic, or because it is obscured by the mouthpiece, or even perhaps because it is hidden deep in the very muscles of the embouchure itself. At any rate, these troubles are very difficult to detect by sight. But as music is intended for the ear, hearing is our best means for discovering these tiny embouchure flaws. I sometimes think that a brass teacher deprived of his eyesight could continue his teaching career, perhaps even more successfully, relying solely on what he *heard* as a guide to correction. For every embouchure fault produces a characteristic deviation from the normal, pure instrumental tone. We have only to learn from experience which fault causes which deviation and we have the problem half solved. The other half will consist of breaking old habits, establishing new and correct procedures, and persevering in these procedures until they become firm habits.

The Angle at Which the Lips are Held

The first of these fine points we should consider is the angle of the lips to the air-stream going through them. It is possible to pout the lips into the mouthpiece and it is equally possible to curl them back over the teeth. We must consider what would constitute a good compromise between these two extremes.

One of the more common misuses of the embouchure is a tendency to protrude the lips out into the mouthpiece—a sort of pouting expression which causes the *inside* surfaces of the lips to become the vibratory edges of the embouchure opening. See Fig. 15. Characteristically, the tone resulting from this is thick, dark, smokey, without ring or reso-

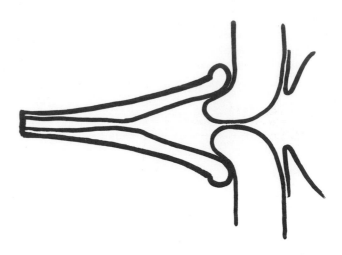

Fig. 15. Incorrect. Lips protruding into mouthpiece.

nance, and inclined to be "grainy", or slightly rough. It gives the impression that all the air is not being converted to vibration—and this is precisely the case.

Let us for a moment consider vibration in general. Ideally, a vibrating surface or vibrating string is set into motion by a force working at a right angle (90°) to its surface or linear direction. A violin bow should cross the strings at right angles. The tympani sticks strike the tympani head at right angles. And even the schoolboy, seeking to annoy the teacher by squeaking his chalk on the blackboard, will instinctively hold the chalk exactly perpendicular to the board. If he "drags" the chalk so that it slants backward to the contact point no vibration will result. Although the school teacher may not fully appreciate his ability to vibrate the chalk, this same type of vibration is a most desirable quality for the brass player to achieve with his lips. If the lips are slanted into the mouthpiece by pouting, the vibration, if it does not stop completely, will be of inferior quality. This results, of course, from the lips not being held in that all-important right angle position to the moving air-stream. The cure consists simply of holding the lips back against the teeth firmly so that they cannot pout. See Fig. 16.

As in all other phases of brass playing, this holding-back feeling is not violent or intense. It is no more, perhaps, than the refusal to permit a pout. Anyone using the cheeks correctly will find that there is very little tendency to pout, as the cheek contraction, opposing, as it does, the lip contraction, draws the lips quite firmly over the arch of the front teeth, successfully preventing the lips from pouting. So, in correcting this inclination to pout into the mouthpiece, give careful consideration to

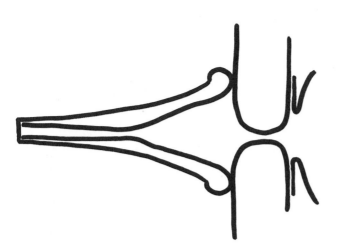

Fig. 16. Correct. Lips held at right angles to mouthpiece.

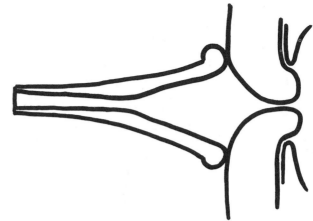

Fig. 17. Incorrect. Lips pulled back over teeth.

the cheek muscles and see that they are doing their share of the work. For, if they are contracting sufficiently, the tendency to let the lips sag into the mouthpiece is practically nil.

In all embouchure problems, overcorrection is as bad as no correction at all. If, in training a tightrope walker, you corrected his tendency to fall always to his right by suggesting that he fall to the left from that time on, he would be little better off. Brass playing and tightrope walking are very much alike, in that a perfect balance requires that we "lean" neither too far left nor too far right.

From the foregoing warning against "pouting", it is conceivable that some students will say to themselves, "I'll fix that problem once and for all by pulling the lips back until they curve in over the teeth like those of an oboe player!" The result of this would be even more detrimental to good brass playing than the pout. See Fig. 17. Here is what happens when the lips slant backward even the slightest degree: The air pressure blowing against the lips tries to swing the lips out, and the little opening so necessary to forming a clear, free tone is actually blown shut. If we imagine a little pair of swinging doors in place of the lips, we shall understand why this undesirable action takes place. Let us suppose that these swinging doors actually touch each other when they are in alignment. See Fig. 18, diagram A. Now, if air is forced out through them, they will swing *outward*. As they do so, the edges, which were just touching, separate, and the opening between them gets larger and larger as the air pressure is increased. See Fig. 18, diagram B. However, if the doors are slanted slightly *inward* before the air pressure is applied, the commencement of the air pressure swings the doors *closed*.

See Fig. 18, diagram C. The inward slanted lips will act in exactly the same manner, producing the most undesirable condition of closing tighter and tighter as we try to play louder and louder. Players who get the feeling that the horn chokes up as they try to make a *crescendo* would do well to explore the possibility that both lips, or even just one, might be held in just such a back-slanted position.

Lower Lip Discipline

The lower lip would seem to be more often the offender. Perhaps it is because the surfaces of the lower teeth, being smaller, offer it less support than the upper teeth offer the upper lip. Or perhaps the lower jaw, tending to recede as it does, allows the lower lip to slide back of the upper lip and thus create a new bad habit. I have had success in solving this problem, once it is definitely established that it *is* the lower lip which is curling in, by the procedure outlined in the following.

First, we must understand that the lower lip is most remarkably agile—much more so than the upper. Its construction permits it to roll very far outward so that it appears large and pouted. Or it can be rolled back inward so that no red shows at all. Because of this we might say that the lower lip has the ability to swivel, exposing at will the finest thin red line or the utmost fullness, including even the inner surface. This flexibility is another reason why we so often find the lower lip rolled or slanted too far back. Luckily, however, this same flexibility makes the correction of the problem relatively easy. Place the lips in the usual playing position on that invaluable aid, the mouthpiece rim, and, using the mirror, observe the proportion of

A	B	C
Swinging doors just touch in alignment.	Air-current swings doors outward. As the current gets stronger, the doors open wider.	Inward slanted doors are blown more and more tightly shut as current gets stronger.

Fig. 18.

each lip being used. Then, without moving or disturbing the upper lip in any way, deliberately take the lower lip out of the rim and replace it lower on the rim. In other words put *less* lower lip into the mouthpiece. This will result in too large an opening between the lips--one which could not possibly vibrate.

Now, without sliding either lip on the mouthpiece rim, *roll* the lower lip farther into the mouthpiece. The flesh of the lower lip will then fill in this too large opening, and, with proper judgment, make the opening just right in size. Note that the lower lip is now exposing slightly more of its inner surface. This procedure might be put in another way. Place the upper lip as always, but deliberately place the mouthpiece a *little* too *high* on the lower lip; then slightly (please note that "slightly") turn the lower lip inside-out until the proper amount of lower lip is again showing in the mouthpiece rim. It will appear to be the same amount as always, *but* the actual playing surface will consist of more of the inner area of the lower lip.

In seeking the necessary moderation in applying this somewhat abstract principle, let us keep well in mind that we are not attempting to pout the lower lip *outward* to a noticeable degree, but only to keep it from rolling *inward* to a detrimental degree. See Figs. 19A and 19B. This entire concept must be tried experimentally with the utmost delicacy and finesse, lest we "lean" too far in the other direction.

As an aside, it might be of interest to the reader to learn that the horn players of a hundred years ago used a lip setting on the mouthpiece which required such an extreme application of this outward rolling of the lower lip that it appeared as though the lower lip was actually out of the mouthpiece and even encompassing some of the mouthpiece beyond and outside the rim. See Fig. 20. Because of its appearance in Germany, this embouchure setting was called *einsetzen* ("setting-in"). This contrasted with the embouchure of the trumpet players of that time and of most modern brass players today--a "setting-on" position, called in Germany, *ansetzen*. Although this old "setting-in" position gave every appearance of employing no lower lip in the mouthpiece, such was not the case. Most of the lower lip was outside the mouthpiece, but the lip was so rolled inside-out that quite a substantial amount of lower lip was in fact present in the mouthpiece. The proportions were much the same as they are for modern horn players: two-thirds upper lip and one-third lower lip. See Fig. 20. The difference lay in the *part* of the lower lip used. The old "setting-in" method used the soft, always moist, inner surface of the lower lip. Although this had some drawbacks, its chief advantages were an extremely soft, mellow tone, and smooth, liquid-like slurs.

Our modern "setting-on" method loses some of

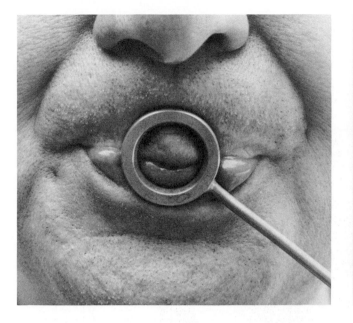 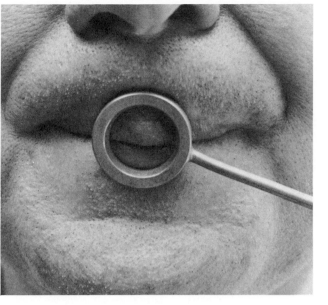

Fig. 19A. Lower lip rolled out too far. Incorrect.   Fig. 19B. Lower lip pulled in too far. Incorrect.

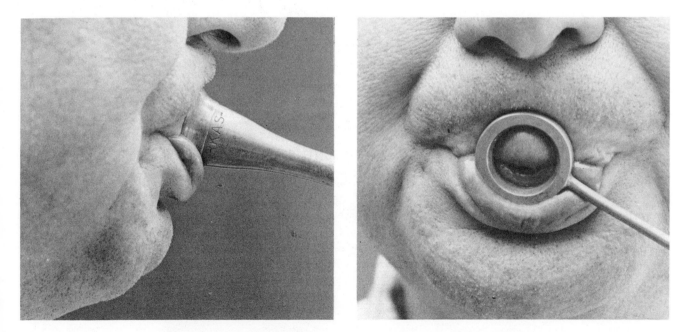

Fig. 20. Front and side view of "setting-in" embouchure (Einsetzen).

this tone and produces a harder, less liquid slur, but gives better endurance, easier high notes and greater technique. Though we use this modern "setting-on" method almost exclusively today, the two methods are not so diametrically opposed as their names might indicate. There has always been a

suggestion of that "setting-in" usage of the lower lip in the "setting-on" embouchure, and it is this *spirit* or *feeling* of similarity, however slight, that I have tried to convey in this discourse concerning the lower lip.

CHICAGO SYMPHONY ORCHESTRA (1959–60)

Conductor Fritz Reiner

The brass players featured in the next chapter are all members of the Chicago Symphony Orchestra. An appreciation of their skill and artistry, not only as individuals but as a superlative brass section, can be obtained by a study of many of the excellent Victor records made recently by Fritz Reiner and the orchestra. Here is a short list of some of the records of particular interest to brass players:

Brahms: Symphony No. 3, Victor LM 2209, LSC 2209; Stravinsky: Baiser de la Fee, Victor LM 2251, LSC 2251; Mahler: Lied von der Erde, Victor LM 6087, LSC 6087; Mahler: Symphony No. 4, Victor LM 2364, LSC 2364; Mussorgsky: Pictures at an Exhibition, Victor LM 2201, LSC 2201; Prokofiev: Lt. Kije Suite, Victor LM 2150, LSC 2150; R. Strauss: Ein Heldenleben, Victor LM 1870; R. Strauss: Don Quixote, Victor LS 2384, LSS 2384; R. Strauss: Don Juan, Victor LM 2462, LSC 2462; Wagner: Rhine Journey, etc. LM 2441, LSC 2441.

2. Photographic Studies of Virtuoso Players

On the following six pages are photographs of members of the Chicago Symphony Orchestra's brass section. Many of the world's greatest conductors have praised this group as an aggregation of some of the finest brass players to be found in the world. These men are from many parts of the country and have studied with many different teachers. Therefore, the similarities in the way they play result because certain fundamental rules of brass playing are observed by successful players, regardless of where or with whom they have studied.. To illustrate this fact, I have chosen to photograph this particular group, not only because each player is an artist of the highest caliber, but also because it is a long established group, and not one that I could be suspected of assembling for the purpose of demonstrating my own pet theories. Regardless of the instrument played, we can observe many important similarities among these fine artists.

1.) The similar mouthpiece placement for players of the same instrument.

2.) The arched-down chins.

3.) The slight thrust of the lower jaws.

4.) The similar angle at which all the instruments are held.

5.) The avoidance of stretched lips.

6.) The slight pucker, as evidenced by the small vertical wrinkles in the lips.

7.) The evidence of taut cheek muscles, which are "trying to smile," in spite of the puckered lips.

8.) Finally, that important basic appearance of general strength—the "brass player's face."

In the course of this book, as various ideas on brass playing are discussed, refer to these photographs and see if these ideas are not very evident in this group of *virtuoso* professional players.

The embouchure techniques revealed by these photographs are sometimes very jealously guarded secrets, and the willingness of these men to reveal these techniques by posing for photographs to be printed in a book offered to the public, is a tribute to their greatness, not only as players, but as teachers. The really great teachers are not only willing, but are eager to help the student by divulging these facets of a complicated art.

Therefore, it is with deepest gratitude that I thank the following men of the Chicago Symphony Orchestra for their generosity in contributing to a most important part of this book.

Adolph Herseth
Rudolph Nashan
Frank Kaderabek
Vincent Cichowicz
Joseph Mourek
Wayne Barrington
Clyde Wedgwood
Robert Lambert
Frank Crisafulli
Edward Kleinhammer
Arnold Jacobs

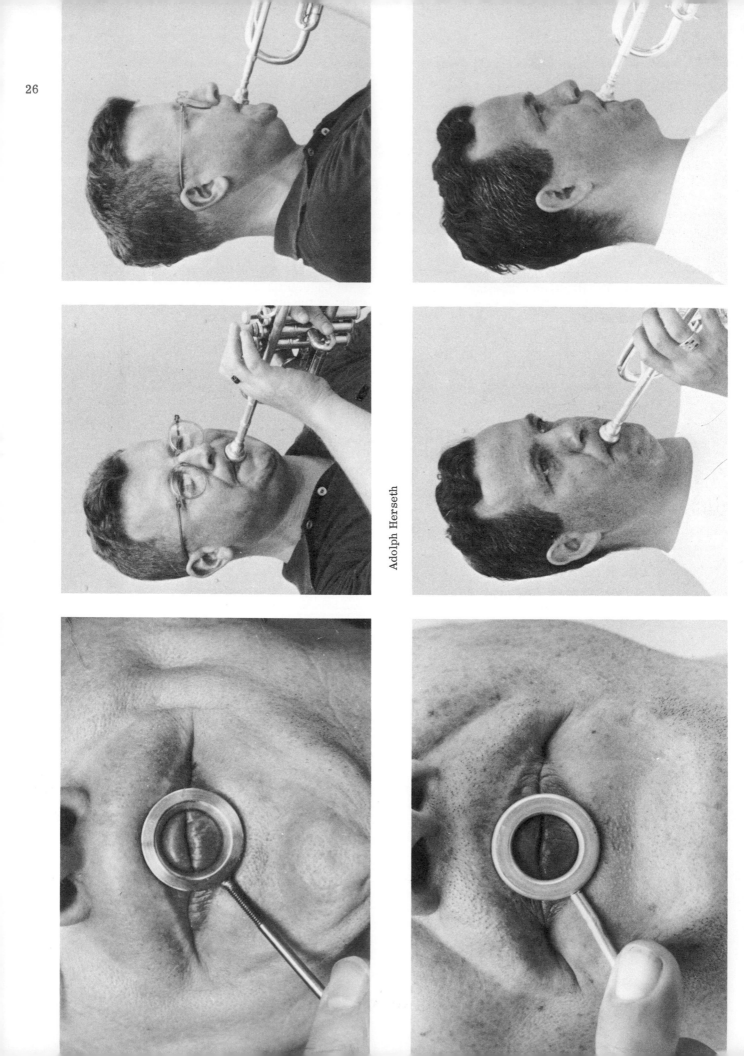

Adolph Herseth

Rudolph Nashan

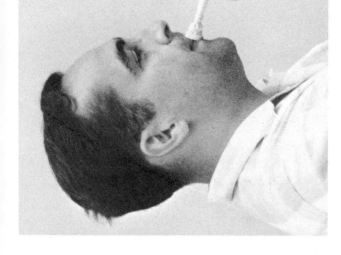

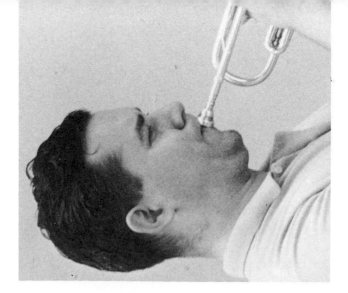

27

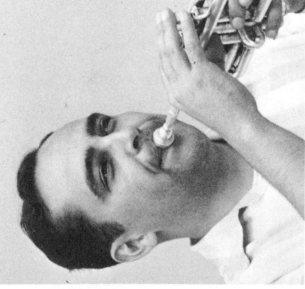

Frank Kaderabek

Vincent Cichowicz

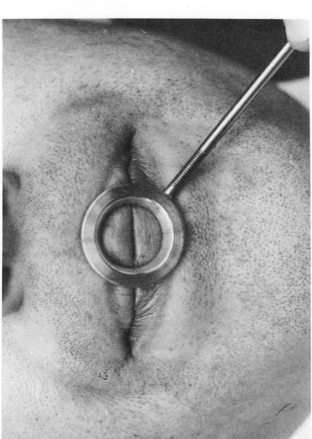

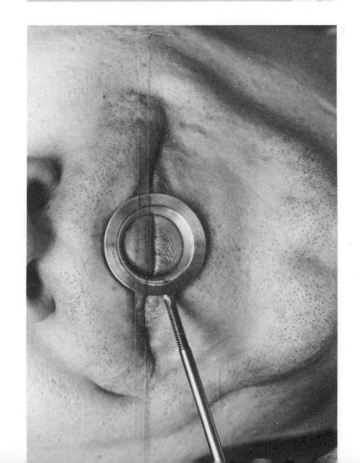

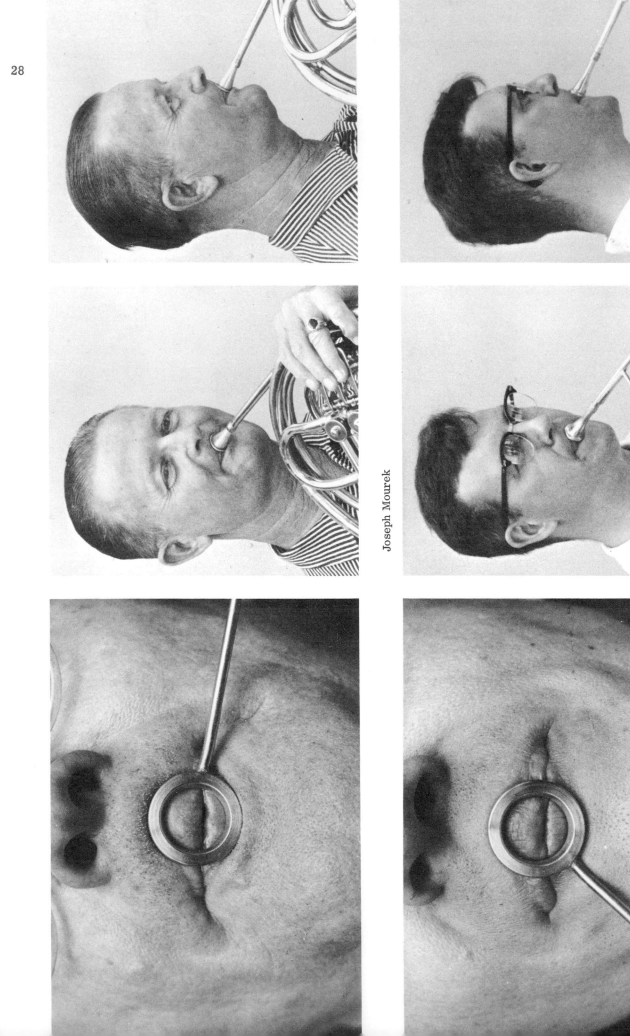

Joseph Mourek

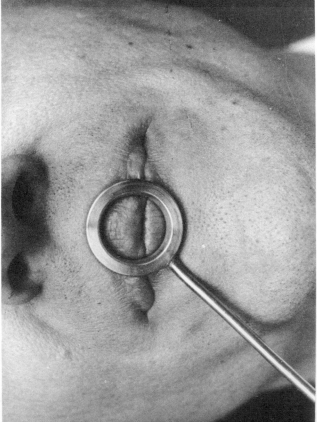

Wayne Barrington

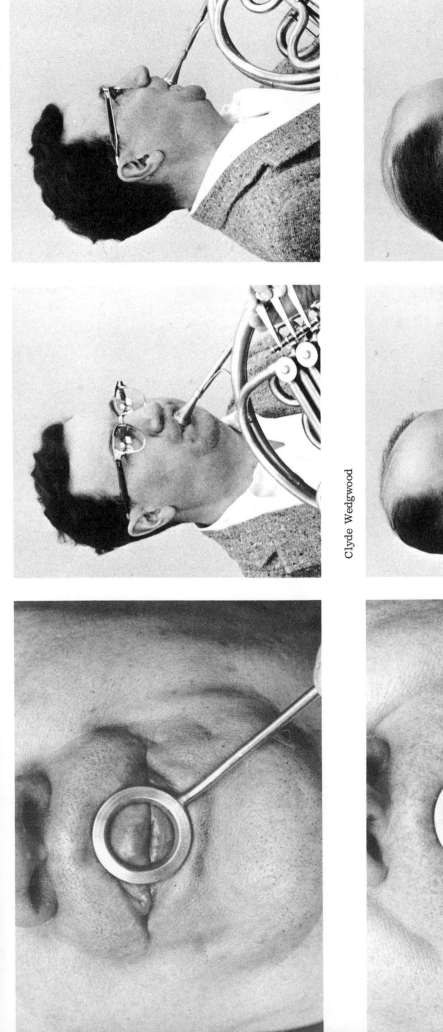

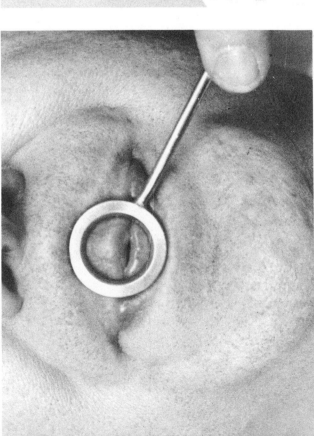

Clyde Wedgwood

Philip Farkas

29

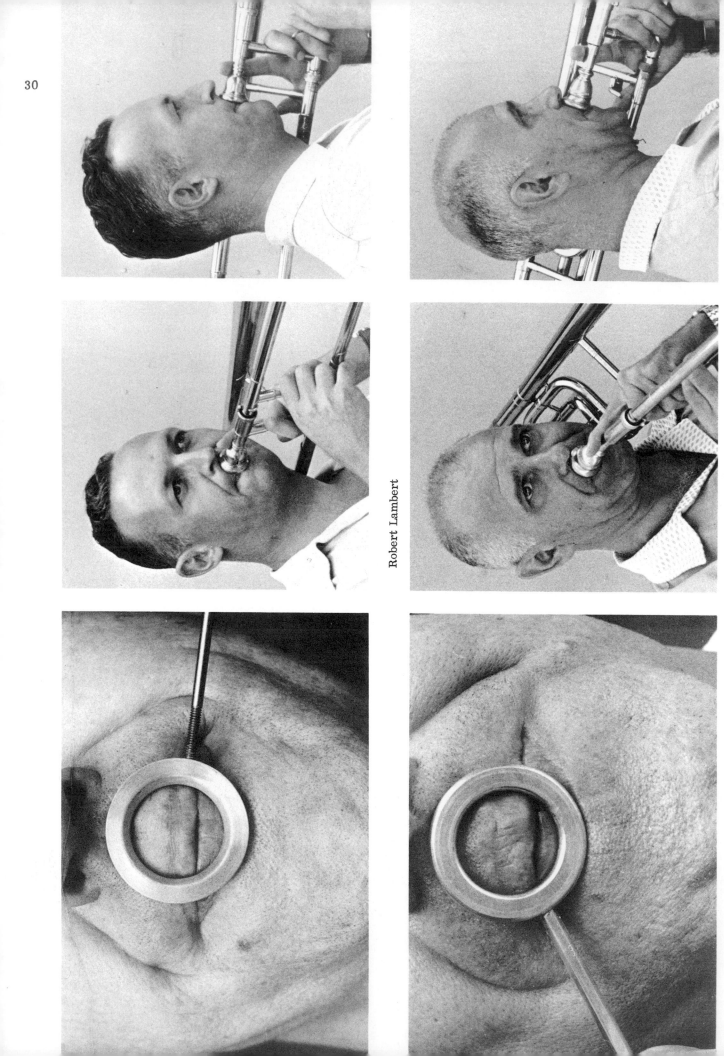

Robert Lambert

Frank Crisafulli

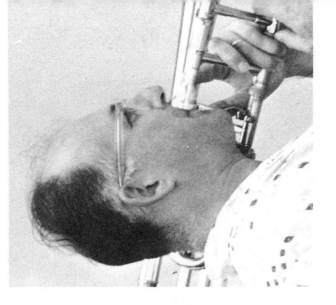

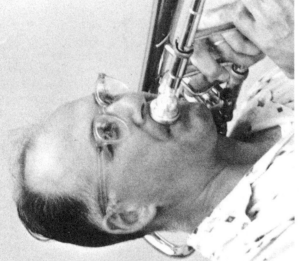

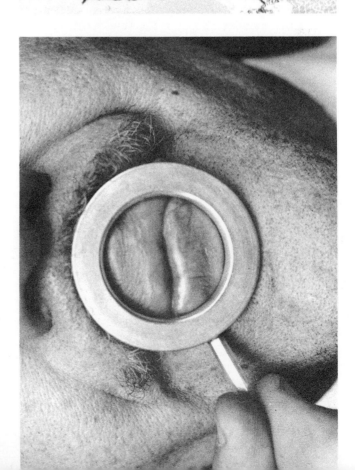

Edward Kleinhammer

Arnold Jacobs

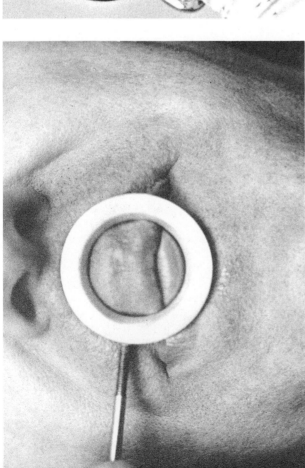

3. Mouthpiece Placement

One of the puzzles of brass playing has always been to find the most advantageous position for placing the mouthpiece on the lips. Perhaps it has not been puzzling *enough* to many players, for there is a remarkably large number of players who have seemingly never given mouthpiece placement the slightest consideration, but have simply "slapped" the mouthpiece up to the lips and commenced blowing. The law of averages, of course, will produce a certain proportion of players who luckily hit the "perfect" spot the first time and proceed to develop this placement into a habit. These players then feel encouraged to tell their pupils, "Go ahead, just put the mouthpiece up to the lips and play."

Of course, the pupil might be equally lucky and hit the perfect position, too. But the odds are against it. Therefore, it seems very wise to give much thoughtful consideration to the exact positioning of the mouthpiece. To complicate matters, no two people will find the same placement ideal. But there is a certain discernable pattern if one will study enough method books and look at enough embouchures. Each type of brass instrument seems to respond noticeably better to one particular lip position, which enables us to formulate a *general* lip setting for that particular instrument.

The proportion of the upper and lower lip on the mouthpiece was probably not worked out in any scientific manner, but is a formula resulting from years of trial-and-error by hundreds of players. In the interest of more rapid and more certain progress, the brass student would be foolish not to take advantage of these thousands of hours of experimentation, and adopt a tried and proven lip position from the very beginning. Then, in the light of his progress, he could make his own personal adjustments. If brass students (and teachers) were more careful about this initial placement of the lips on the mouthpiece, there would be no need for all of the experimentation and frustrating adjustment that we find today. It is so much easier to place the mouthpiece correctly for the beginner, with his flaccid lips and lack of preconceived ideas, than it is to break old and firmly established bad habits in a student of even a few months.

French Horn Mouthpiece Placement

For the French horn this formula requires two-thirds upper lip and one-third lower lip in the mouthpiece. I have seen this statement made in perhaps two dozen horn methods, some very modern, some written back in the late 1700's. I have two books on the playing of the hunting horn--which is, after all, the direct ancestor of the modern horn. Both these books advocate the use of two-thirds upper lip and one-third lower lip. Encouraged by such unanimity of opinion, from experts covering a span of almost two hundred years, I decided to investigate why and *if* this two-thirds, one-third proportion is necessary. During this investigation I have photographed several dozen horn players' embouchures as seen in playing position through the rim-on-a-stick. Naturally, to arrive at any logical conclusion, only the highest quality professional players were included. *Without exception*, these photographs showed the approximate proportion of two-thirds upper lip and one-third lower lip. Of course, this proportion is not mathematically exact, nor did the players show *identical* positions. But the *general* lip placement could be adequately described as two-thirds upper and one-third lower lip. There was a pronounced difference in the amount of lower lip used between the player using the *most* and the player using the *least* lower lip. But *all* the players used a considerably larger amount of upper lip than lower. I have never met a really accomplished French horn player who used *more* lower lip than upper. Such players might exist, but they are in such a small minority that certainly no thoughtful student or teacher would deviate from the tried-and-true "two-thirds upper lip" method without some serious and compelling physical reason. The only reason serious enough to warrant such a deviation would be a malformation of jaw, teeth, or lips. Even then, a person with a malformation pronounced enough to make such a consideration necessary is probably ill-advised to study any brass instrument, let alone French horn. The brass family presents enough problems to even the most perfectly adapted student. Besides, there are so many other soul-satisfying musical instruments available that it does seem most logical to consider your physical assets and liabilities before choosing anything as important as the instrument to which you may very well devote thousands of hours (not to mention dollars!) during the course of your lifetime.

Let me sum up the evidence which leads me to conclude that two-thirds upper and one-third lower lip in the mouthpiece are a prerequisite for the

French horn player who wishes to attain his maximum ability.

First, most of the fine French horn teachers of the past two hundred years have advocated this position. Many of these teachers have written instruction books which substantiate this statement. Second, *all* of the many fine horn players that I know personally (perhaps one hundred or more) use this predominantly upper lip setting. Twelve photos of such embouchures appear in my book, *The Art of French Horn Playing.** Four are included in this book. Incidently, I have not eliminated any photos which did not conform to this theory. I didn't have to. All the photographs consistently showed the same relative setting. Third, believing and preaching this theory for years has resulted in a number of my students becoming professional players in many of our finest symphony orchestras.

There is good reason why the successful French horn player finds it necessary to adopt this two-thirds upper, one-third lower lip position. Of all the brass instrument embouchures, the horn player's is probably the softest, most relaxed and most puckered. This tends to emphasize the heavy, fleshy mound in the center of the upper lip. With this mound as pronounced as it is, it is logical for the French horn player to place the mouthpiece *above* it rather than try to perch the rim precariously *upon* it. The thicker condition of the upper lip, when it is the dominating lip in the mouthpiece, seems to give the tone a more mellow, less strident quality. And, of course, this velvety quality is much to be desired in the French horn tone.

Trumpet and Cornet Mouthpiece Placement

As in the case of French horn players, the great trumpet and cornet virtuosi and teachers of the past century and a half have advocated a certain, fairly exact positioning of the lips on the mouthpiece. (In discussing this further we will include the cornet whenever mention is made of the trumpet, as they are identical, at least in the consideration of mouthpiece placement.) Although the majority of French horn teachers favor the proportion of two-thirds upper lip to one-third lower lip in the mouthpiece, the great preponderance of famous trumpet teachers advocate exactly the opposite proportion for their instrument. Two-thirds *lower* lip and one-third *upper* lip in the mouthpiece is, almost without exception, the rule of the best-known teachers. Just to name a very few, this proportion of upper and lower lip is stressed in the books of Arban, St. Jacome, Vincent Bach and Max Schlossberg.

*Published by Summy-Birchard Publishing Co., Evanston, Ill., 1956.

There are several reasons for the trumpet player's need of two-thirds lower and one-third upper lip in the mouthpiece. As would be expected, they are related to the horn player's reasons, but are the result of almost entirely reverse requirements. As the trumpet player, in order to produce a ringing, brilliant tone, must keep his lips in a tenser, perhaps less puckered embouchure than the horn player, the mound of flesh in the center of the upper lip is not nearly so evident. In fact, this prominence is inclined to be held back against the teeth so firmly, that it is actually less in evidence than when the lips are in repose. As there is no hump, there is no need to place the mouthpiece above it.

The two-thirds upper lip position for the French horn allows the fleshy mound of the upper lip to more or less protrude into the mouthpiece a slight distance, resulting in a mellowing effect on the tone. However, even though the trumpet player's two-third *lower* lip position represents the same proportion as the horn player's *upper* lip position, the tonal result is quite different. Each of us has a fairly fleshy lower lip, but in contrast to the upper lip, it has no protrusion or hump in the center. In fact, there is usually a shallow concavity in the center. When the trumpet mouthpiece is set against it, the lower lip, even though it is in greater evidence, is pressed flat and has very little tendency to protrude into the mouthpiece. This, of course, aids in producing the desired brilliance. So we see that in spite of the natural assumption that two-thirds of either lip in the mouthpiece should produce similar tonal results, because of this *difference in shape* of the two lips, such is not the case. For the horn player, the fleshy and relatively soft mound of the upper lip achieves the soft quality he desires. But the hardness he would produce in the horn tone, were he to use two-thirds lower lip, is just the ideal condition for achieving a beautiful ringing trumpet tone. From these observations we can see that this two-thirds lower lip position is not just an arbitrary setting, but one based on logical conclusions resulting from many years of trial and error.

Trombone and Baritone Mouthpiece Placement

As with all the other brass instruments, there is a preferred placement of the lips on the trombone or baritone mouthpiece. However, although lip placement is remarkably consistent among horn and trumpet players, it is not nearly so consistent among trombone players. (We will include the baritone in this discussion whenever reference is made to the trombone.) Many fine trombonists seem to prefer the two-thirds upper, one-third lower lip position. However, there are just enough excellent players who play with more lower than upper lip to prevent our formulating any strict rule about the necessity of this two-thirds upper lip placement. Perhaps this is due to the size of the trombone mouthpiece. Since trumpet and horn mouthpieces are relatively small, a sixteenth of an inch misplacement of the lips can represent, percentagewise, enough discrepancy to produce very unsatisfactory playing results. On the other hand, because of the very size of the trombone mouthpiece, a sixteenth of an inch variation in placement might cause very little difference in the playing results. In some ways this is analogous to the contrast between a violin string and a contrabass string. If the violinist miscalculates the placement of a finger for a high note by as little as a sixteenth of an inch, the influence on his intonation can be quite critical. Yet the bass player would find that a full half-inch misplacement of his finger causes less intonation trouble than that experienced by the violinist.

The above does not mean that the trombonist can usually place the mouthpiece anywhere on his mouth and get equally good results. However, it does mean that he has more choice of lip positions which are seemingly successful. This is all the more reason to choose, through experience, experimenting, and plain logic, the very best position for one's own best results. Sometimes a little *controlled, methodical* experimenting can advance one's playing overnight far more than months of persistent practice on a less desirable lip setting.

Tuba Mouthpiece Placement

Much the same latitude of mouthpiece placement is found among tuba players as is found among trombonists. If there seems to be more consistency in placement among tuba players, it is perhaps because the large mouthpiece is stopped in its upward travel when the top of the rim touches the nose! Just as the trombonist's lip placement is less critical than the trumpeter's, because of the larger mouthpiece, the placement of the tuba player's lips is less criti-

cal than the placement of the trombonist's. I use this word "critical" in its meaning of actual measurable distance. I believe that the horn or trumpet player must certainly come within a sixteenth of an inch of his own "ideal spot" for superior results. The trombonist has, perhaps, an eighth of an inch of latitude for the same quality result. But the tuba player might succeed even with his mouthpiece a quarter of an inch higher or lower than that hypothetical "ideal spot." This does not imply that the tuba player can carelessly place the mouthpiece anywhere on his lips. The "ideal spot" produces such superior results in all phases of playing that the tuba player is well justified in spending some experimental time seeking it.

Summary

There is no difficulty in recognizing this "ideal spot", as the results are usually quite startling. The transition from high to low register and vice versa suddenly becomes easy. The tonguing becomes cleaner and the tone richer. Even the need for pressure is reduced.

But there is another important reason to find and recognize this ideal position of the mouthpiece—to gain consistency. All brass players experience a difference in their day-to-day performance ability. Some of this is undoubtedly due to the changing condition of the lips, as a result of fatigue, chapped lips, lack of practice, etc. However, most of our inconsistent playing is the result of inconsistent lip placement. This inconsistent placement may be the result of two things: the mouthpiece may be placed differently on the lips each time, out of sheer carelessness; or it may be placed, purposely or subconsciously, on a new spot to avoid setting it on tired, sore muscles.

Thus, the experiment of seeking and finding the ideal spot to place the mouthpiece will not only improve the tone and technique, but will also, when consistently used, lead to consistent, accurate playing.

4. Moist Versus Dry Lips

Strangely, one of the most important playing details which should concern the brass player is seldom taught, discussed or found in writing. It is the decision each player must, consciously or unconsciously, make for himself as to whether he should keep his lips moist or dry while playing—for his own best results. All of us instinctively know that the decision is important, as all of us have, at one time or another, heard brass players complain in this vein: "I was very nervous during the concert last night and my lips got so dry I could hardly play a note." And the opposite complaint: "It was so hot on the stage that the perspiration ran down my face and the mouthpiece slid all over my lips." Now each player had a legitimate complaint and yet each would have welcomed the very condition that spoiled the other's performance. Let us discuss both lip conditions and see if one might be preferable to the other. There are fine players in each category, and undoubtedly they can give good and logical reasons why their particular use of wet or dry lips is best for them. However, after many years of observation, I have concluded that a large majority of brass players—I would estimate about seventy-five per cent—prefer to keep their lips moist while playing. This is my own preference and I would find it most disconcerting to try to start playing on dry lips. Nevertheless, the minority group would undoubtedly feel just as uncomfortable if required to change to wet lips.

The arguments presented by the dry-lip advocates are usually these. The mouthpiece "stays put" on the lips without any tendency to slip around; in other words, the mouthpiece sticks to the lips. Furthermore, this stickiness enables the player to brace the lips against the mouthpiece and thus aid the production of high notes. There are probably several other good reasons which I, as a non-believer, do not appreciate, and the considerable ability of some of the dry-lip advocates lends weight to these reasons. But as an advocate of the wet-lip school, I would like to present a variety of reasons for preferring it, and should start, perhaps, by stating my objections to the dry-lip method. Here are these objections roughly in the order of their importance:

1. When the mouthpiece is touched to the dry lips, it tends to stick at the exact spot it first touches, making any maneuvering to that so-called "ideal spot" quite difficult.

2. The very act of bracing the dry lips against the mouthpiece for aid in obtaining high notes acts as a crutch in preventing the most complete development of the lips. Should the lips inadvertently become moist, they will slip out of the mouthpiece upon attempting high notes, not having the *inherent* strength to obtain them without that "crutch"—that necessity to adhere themselves to the mouthpiece rim.

3. There are times when the lips are going to become moist, whether this condition is wanted or not. A hot summer day or intense stage lighting can bring out enough perspiration on the face to make the mouthpiece slippery against the lips. Often the very act of playing conveys enough moisture on the air stream to moisten the lips. The dry-lip player finds himself in a dilemma during these situations, one which can bring on a "sweat", aggravating this slippery condition even more. I have watched famous jazz trumpet players—the so-called "screechers"—who play several octaves above the normal trumpet range. Many of them have to dry their lips carefully with a towel (or sleeve!) every time they have a few bars rest. Considering the ridiculously high (or should I say *marvelously* high) range they accomplish, perhaps this is a necessity. But it must be remembered that this very high playing is heard but infrequently in the course of an evening, and what works very well for intermittent playing, might not be at all practical for the normal-range player, who plays continually, and will not find frequent enough rests in his playing to apply the towel.

4. Occasionally some brass player develops an ugly sore or raw spot on his lips at the point where the mouthpiece makes contact. His complaint is usually that this lesion does not heal as long as he continues to play his instrument. Only complete cessation of playing for several weeks will bring about a healing. Naturally, this is a serious situation for a professional player. If he rests, he is not earning; if he continues to play, he is ham-

pered by the ever-present sore. The worst of it is that the vacation brings only temporary relief, and continued playing could produce something much more ominous than the simple sore. The entire point of this unpleasant little discussion is that I have never encountered a brass player with this type of lip sore who played on wet lips. Invariably these plagued players use the dry-lip method. The constant applying and removing of the mouthpiece from dry lips, with its attendant tiny, but apparent pulling sensation as the mouthpiece parts from the lips, can finally cause an abrasion to the skin, which once started gets increasingly worse. This is not to imply that everyone who performs on dry lips will sooner or later develop a sore. Actually this condition is rarely found among brass players, but, when it is found, it is always the *dry-lip* advocate who is the victim. I have helped several students who had persistent lip sores by simply insisting that they change from a dry-lip to a moist-lip procedure. Lubrication is supplied by the simple act of lightly touching the tongue to the lip surfaces and to the mouthpiece rim before each setting-on of the mouthpiece. This successfully stops the pulling action of the mouthpiece against the skin of the lips each time the mouthpiece is removed, and in a week or two complete healing takes place. Best of all, no lay-off is required. A great deal of patience is needed while the new procedure is learned, but this does not indicate that the method itself is wrong, as I am sure that changing from a *wet* lip to a *dry* lip would cause an equal amount of discouragement during the transitional stage.

The above paragraphs amplify my reasons for rejecting the dry-lip method. This, of course, is the *negative* approach to my preference for the moist lip. Following are some of the *positive* reasons for this preference.

1. With the ability of the mouthpiece to slide on the lips, a very accurate positioning of the lips can be achieved. Just at the moment the wet-lip player puts his mouthpiece into position on his lips, he very quickly and almost unnoticeably flicks his moist tongue over his lips and the mouthpiece rim, which is, by this time, only a fraction of an inch from the lips. At first, this process must be developed very consciously, but after a short while it will become almost a reflex action—as natural as inhaling before an attack. When the lips are highly trained, they build and develop muscle around the mouthpiece rim, giving the player the feeling of a definite groove into which the mouthpiece rim will fit. The slippery condition of the lips enables the player to make minute adjustments in this placement, dictated by comfort, intuition, and carefully developed knowledge of the best placement.

2. The wet-lip system requires one to develop the lip muscles. When the dry-lip player "tucks" a lot of lip into the mouthpiece, it sticks in place and thus creates the tight, small lip opening needed for high notes, but in an artificial manner. Dry lips used for high notes are just a crutch, employed instead of completely developing the muscles. The biggest objection voiced by the dry-lip advocate when first experimenting with the wet-lip procedure results from his feeling of great weakness in reaching the high notes. He cannot get a "grip" on the mouthpiece with his lips. In fact, the higher he attempts to play, the more he feels that the lips are about to slip out from under the mouthpiece altogether. This is, I believe, simply an indication that the lips have not been completely developed muscularly, or at least have not been trained in the right manner. But if the player would slowly and carefully develop his playing ability on moist lips, first in the low and middle registers, and then, little by little, work into the higher register, he would develop strength in muscles heretofore unused. Finally he would gain a completely developed embouchure—one which could attain high notes with a minimum of pressure and with the embouchure's own inherent strength to "focus down" on a small, strong, high-pitched vibration stream, with no external aid.

3. As mentioned in point number 4 of my *objections* to the dry lip, I have never found, in a player who keeps his lips lubricated, a lip sore caused by the mouthpiece. These sores are relatively rare and concern very few of even the dry-lip players. But all of us are concerned occasionally by *chapped* lips, and here again I feel that the wet-lip player has the advantage. When the player using dry lips has to play on chapped lips, the thick, dead skin, which *also* must be kept dry, creates a very sluggish, vibrationless embouchure. But the wet-lip advocate, constantly moistening his lips, as he must, finally, even though it may take many minutes, succeeds in soaking this heavy, dead membrane.

If this moistening does not quite bring the lips up to their usual flexible condition, it at least makes them far more flexible than the completely dry, parchment-like skin which the dry-lip player will have to endure for several days. We brass players like to compare our lips to the reeds used by the woodwinds. Perhaps we should carry the analogy further and moisten our "reed", as would any good woodwind player when he expects it to perform with the utmost flexibility and efficiency.

The fact that the lips start to dry and stick to the mouthpiece during a long continued musical passage will not cause concern when it is borne in mind that the moisture on the lips has served its purpose once the lips have been accurately positioned and the passage begun. The sensation of progressive drying can be quite disconcerting and yet cause no musical trouble. We who use the wet-lip method become so accustomed to avoiding any stickiness when applying the mouthpiece, that we often experience, during an extended passage, a very strong compulsion to stop momentarily and lick the lips. In spite of this sometimes irresistable urge, the practice of continuing unwaveringly onward will develop the assurance that drying lips are not detrimental *once the mouthpiece is correctly placed and playing begun.*

5. The Lip Aperture

Without doubt, the ultimate object of all the muscular development, mouthpiece positioning, jaw setting, lip moistening, etc., is to form an aperture between the lips, of the right size, shape and firmness. This small opening between the lips, in the final analysis, takes complete command over the air-column's vibration and is therefore the determining factor in the brass instrumentalist's playing ability. All the previous embouchure rules, suggestions and exercises discussed in this book have been aimed directly at this object of forming the most perfect lip aperture possible. Therefore, a thorough discussion of its shape and size, and of the lip density, will not only clarify the exact objective of all the components making up the embouchure, but will show how each of these components can cooperate in attaining this goal.

The open end of the oboe reed so closely duplicates the size, shape, and function of the brass player's embouchure aperture that it is ideal for comparison purposes. Have you ever really looked at an oboe reed? If not, make a point of doing so. Exactly like the brass player's embouchure aperture, the oboe reed must have three inherent conditions in order to perform successfully: it must be the right shape; it must be the right size; and it must be made of the right material. Let us discuss these conditions and their similarity to the lip opening.

What Shape Lip Aperture?

The reed is carefully constructed of two pieces of cane which are arched against each other so that the opening at the end of the reed has a very exact and carefully planned shape, thus: ⬳. If the opening is too highly arched, the air does not "rub" the reed and it fails to vibrate. On the other hand, if the opening is too flat, the air "catches" the reed and blows it completely shut. This is the reason we have all occasionally noticed an oboe player scrutinizing the end of his reed and then gently pinching it, either sideways or in an up and down direction. He is vitally interested in that shape, because when it is just right, the reed vibrates to the greatest degree, neither failing to "speak" nor choking up completely.

We have the same problems with our lip aperture. It, too, should have this shape: ⬳. When it is held too flat, the tone of a brass instrument will

sound choked or tight and may even fail to commence at all during a *pianissimo* attack, at which time the air-column is simply too weak to create vibration in the tight and narrow horizontal slot which opposes it.

In contrast, as with the arched-too-open oboe reed, we find the brass player who holds his lip aperture too round and open. This is a much rarer fault than the tight, flat opening, but equally incorrect. Such a player usually has a dark, "hooty" tone—airy and without a ringing quality. In his case, the opening is not resisting the air-column enough and some of the air is getting through the too-highly-arched lip aperture without "rubbing". This player will often have *pianissimo* attacks fail to speak simply because the tiny air-column "sneaks" through the too-large opening without ever touching the edges, so to speak, resulting in no vibration whatever!

Notice that either type of embouchure fault creates most of its problems in *pianissimo* playing. Any embouchure shape will speak if we blast enough air through it. Therefore we must pay a great deal more attention to the ability to play softly and delicately when determining the quality of our own or a student's embouchure.

How do we determine whether the aperture being used is the right shape? And if it is not, what should be done to influence its shape in the right direction? Visual observations can be of some help in determining the correct shape of the lip aperture, although a great deal of experience is needed to ascertain whether it differs or conforms to the average good embouchure. Here again, it might be useful, with the help of the mouthpiece rim and mirror, to compare one's own lip aperture to the embouchure illustrations in this book. The ear, however, is still the best guide in determining what is right or wrong with the embouchure aperture. Of course, if the playing is of superb quality, the less tampering with the embouchure the better. Therefore, we must assume that only those players having difficulties will be interested in this discussion. These difficulties can all be used as clues or symptoms. Here is a list of troubles which usually indicate a too flat embouchure aperture (⬳):

1. *Tight, bright, hard tone.*
   This tone is usually too brittle to be pleasant to the ear. In spite of this over-brilliance,

the tone is generally small in volume and has a constricted quality, a quality which makes the listener instinctively want to "clear his throat."

2. *A tendency to play sharp.*

   This sharping usually shows up most distinctly during soft passages, and occurs in all registers.

3. *Pianissimo attacks which fail to speak.*

   If the cause is too flat an opening, the air has trouble getting through the lips, resulting in a *choked*, small, sizzling sound instead of the note. Or, often the attack is accompanied by a lip resistance which makes the player feel as though he is getting red in the face. When the lips finally part, the sound disconcertingly blurts out louder than wanted.

4. *A sizzling sound, like frying bacon, particularly apparent in long-sustained, soft high notes.*

   This is caused by little "strings" of saliva which bridge the small gap between the lips, especially at the corners of the aperture. These flutter and buzz, interfering with the cleanness of the air column. These saliva strings, being viscid, will stretch just so far and cannot bridge the gap in a properly arched lip aperture. When this arch is high enough, the little strings simply never come into existence, or if they should, they cannot stretch the distance involved and will break at the least breath of air.

5. *Inability to carry a diminuendo down to nothing.*

   The *diminuendo* will continue just so far and then the note suddenly stops vibrating. Often this stopping is preceded by the sizzling sounds described in number 4 above. The note suddenly stops vibrating because the lip opening is too flat. In fact, the only reason that there is an opening at all, in this case, is because air is being forced through it. In the course of a *diminuendo*, when the air force diminishes to a certain point, the lips simply collapse together, completely stopping the note. When the lip aperture is correctly shaped, it is *formed* and not *blown* into this shape. In other words, the correct opening is so formed that even when air is not passing through it, the shape is maintained by the correct use of the muscles involved. Such an opening will not collapse when the air column is carried down to a mere thread, and consequently a *diminuendo* can be brought right down to infinity.

Should any or all of the five preceding symptoms seem applicable to you, it would be prime evidence, in my opinion, that the lip opening is being held too flat. The following corrective measures should be tried, as any one, or a combination of them, might prove to be the solution to this most discouraging flat aperture problem.

1. Make sure that the upper and lower front teeth are sufficiently separated. That is, keep the lower jaw down far enough that some influence is exerted toward arching the center of the lower lip downward. This idea is fully discussed later in the book.

2. Arch the chin muscles down with sufficient strength to make that wide "U" shaped indentation (discussed earlier on page 16) clearly evident. Remember that any small horizontal wrinkle which might appear between the lower lip and the tip of the chin should be stretched completely out of existence by this arching process.

3. Avoid too wide a smile. There is great suspicion, when the lip aperture is too flat, that the cheek muscles are pulling the lips into too tight a smile. In other words, the cheek muscles are *winning* their perpetual tug-of-war with the circular muscle around the mouth (orbicularis oris). This should not be permitted, of course, as we want neither of these sets of muscles to *win*, but simply create tension between each other. The balance, in this case, can be restored by consciously puckering the mouth more, at the same time relaxing the cheek muscles to some degree. In re-establishing this balance, good judgment, as usual, will be needed and the earlier practice of flexing the various facial muscles *separately* will serve to good advantage.

4. Make certain that the corners of the mouth are *kept in* so that the width of the mouth from corner to corner is shorter than when the mouth is smiling. This statement should not be construed as synonymous with the idea expressed in corrective measure No. 3. It is possible to have a nice balance between the cheek muscles and the circular lip muscle and yet have the corners of the mouth, in this balance, suspended *too far apart*. For instance, if one first creates a broad smile, and then, without relinquishing this smile in the slightest, adds the puckering tension of the lip muscles, he will have a well-balanced tension, but with the mouth spread too wide. It would be much more correct for the player

trying to improve the too-flat lip aperture *first* to pucker the lips and *then* add the cheek muscles to balance the tension. This will result in the same balance of tension as the first idea, but with the corners of the mouth considerably closer together, resulting in a more arched-open lip aperture.

Although most faulty embouchure apertures err in the direction of being held or pinched too flat, occasionally we find a player who, by lowering the jaw too much and by puckering the lips to excess, creates an aperture which is too circular or highly arched ($\diamond$). Appearance can be helpful in determining this, but usually the hollow, dull, "furry" tone quality is sufficient evidence. Obviously, the cure for this condition is the *moderate* approach *toward* the opposite (but equally faulty) embouchure— the broad smile and clenched jaw. Perhaps it is more discreet to advise less pucker than to suggest more smile, although the meanings are synonymous in my mind. Parenthetically, how often I have heard two pupils of the same teacher compare notes and discover, with indignation, that each has been given exactly the opposite advice by the teacher. This might seem confusing to the pupil, but the good teacher must give advice which appears to contradict his statements made to another student, perhaps even that very day. My last two suggestions seem to contradict each other. The pupil with the bright, thin, hard tone is told to pucker the corners of the mouth inward while lowering the jaw and arching the chin down, while the student with the dull, hooty, dark tone and (usually) flat intonation is asked to tighten the cheeks more and try to draw the lips into more of a smile, at the same time avoiding lowering the jaw too much. The teacher is not contradicting himself; he simply has in mind an ideal norm between these two extremes and must advise anything which brings the student closer to this norm.

What Size Lip Aperture?

We learn in mathematics that geometric shapes can be compared as being *identical* or *similar*. *Identical* forms are exactly the same *shape* and *size*, while *similar* forms must be *shaped* alike but need *not* necessarily be the same size. While forming the little "oboe reed" opening between our lips, we should keep this meaning of the word "similar" very clearly in mind. That is, we must always keep the lip opening *shaped* like the end of an oboe reed, but the *size* of this opening must vary to a great degree between the highest and lowest notes. I will go a step farther and state that one's total range will depend directly on just how large and how small

he can make that opening. I believe that it is the horizontal *width* of this opening which determines the pitch of the note. Observe the vibration of the lips while buzzing in the rim. There is a fuzzy appearance to both the upper and lower arc of the opening. This blurred look is caused by the high pitched vibration. Here again we can observe the similarity to the oboe reed, because we also have a "double-reed", inasmuch as *both* the upper and lower arcs of the lip opening vibrate—or should, if all the suggestions made are utilized.

There is a simple test which will substantiate the theory that the horizontal width of the aperture determines the pitch of the note. With care we can almost measure the exact width of this vibrating opening, in spite of its blurred appearance. A basic law of acoustics states that if a vibrating object, such as a violin string, is touched at the halfway point in its length, the resulting half-length should sound an octave higher than the full-length pitch. By careful observation this same law can be seen and heard to determine our pitch on any brass instrument. Buzz a middle register note on your mouthpiece rim and with the aid of the mirror, calculate the approximate width of the vibrating opening. Then, at the same volume, buzz an exact octave higher. The opening will become exactly half as wide.

For example:

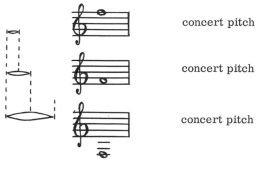

concert pitch

concert pitch

concert pitch

FIG. 21

These approximate lip aperture sizes are calculated for a horn player holding the indicated notes at about a mf level

I have tested this theory with many players and find it always holds true. From this we can derive a simple formula: the higher one wishes to play, the smaller he must make the lip aperture from corner to corner.

Unfortunately, this simple statement is not quite true under all playing conditions, but then nothing is quite as simple in playing an instrument as such basic statements would at first lead one to believe. There is one other important factor beside that of pitch which must be considered in determining the size of this lip aperture, and that is *volume*.

The louder we play, the more air we must use, and the lip aperture must accommodate this air-column. Therefore, we can make another seemingly simple statement regarding the lip aperture: the louder one plays, the larger the lip aperture becomes. This statement may also be proved with the aid of the rim and mirror. Buzz a long-tone, starting *pianissimo* and make a *crescendo* to *fortissimo*, being very careful to keep the pitch steady. The lip opening will become visibly larger as the *crescendo* takes place.

Now we see that our two simple statements combine and modify each other so that together they are not quite so simple. This is not said to confound or worry the brass student. As a matter of fact, nearly all brass players use these facts so instinctively and naturally in their everyday playing that they need give it no thought. But, as this book is written for the player who is having trouble, the *conscious* knowledge of how and why this lip aperture works as it does may supply the needed clue to his lack of range, and volume contrast. When the player fixes this compound fact in mind (the higher we play, the smaller the lip aperture; the louder we play, the larger the lip aperture), he can evolve from it several interesting statements, each of which might help him solve some problem, or hitherto difficult passage.

Here are some statements which can be based on our original premise:

THE *HIGHEST, SOFTEST*, NOTE ONE CAN PLAY IS THE RESULT OF THE SMALLEST LIP APERTURE HE CAN PRODUCE. Just realizing this fact should help the student who lacks a good *pianissimo*, in the high register. THE *LOWEST, LOUDEST NOTE* ONE CAN PLAY WILL REQUIRE THE LARGEST LIP APERTURE HE CAN PRODUCE. Might not this knowledge help the player who cannot get low notes, or, at best, only produce them softly?

A PERFECTLY CALCULATED *CRESCENDO* DURING AN ASCENDING SCALE PASSAGE COULD CONCEIVABLY BE PRODUCED WITH NO CHANGE IN THE SIZE OF THE LIP APERTURE. This would result from the fact that the gradually enlarging aperture due to the *crescendo* is exactly offset by the diminishing aperture caused by the *ascent* in *range*. This knowledge will help the student with a pinched high register to realize that in playing high notes with a full, large tone, one must use copious amounts of air, but must *not* restrict this air with a too-small lip aperture. In fact, he will find that

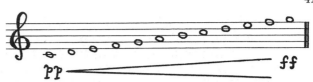

Fig. 22. The ascending notes require a constantly diminishing lip aperture. The increasing volume requires a constantly enlarging lip aperture. Therefore, these two conditions cancel out each other, requiring little or no change in lip aperture size, depending, of course, on the exact amount of crescendo and the range covered.

the lip opening can be kept surprisingly large when high notes are played *forte*.

Conversely, and for the same reasons: A DIMINUENDO DURING A DESCENDING PASSAGE WILL REQUIRE LITTLE OR NO LIP APERTURE CHANGE. Again, this statement should help the

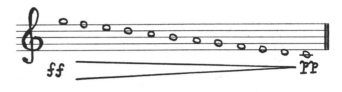

Fig. 23. The descending notes require a constantly enlarging lip aperture. The diminishing volume requires a constantly diminishing lip aperture. Therefore, these two conditions cancel out each other, requiring little or no change in the size of the lip aperture.

student to realize how relatively more important the air production is in this type of passage than any large change in embouchure.

AN ASCENDING PASSAGE REQUIRING A DIMINUENDO WILL NECESSITATE A DRASTIC LIP CONTRACTION DURING THE ASCENT. Just realizing this fact will help the student to focus his

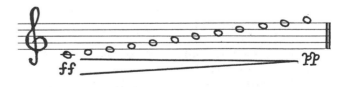

Fig. 24. The ascending notes require a constantly diminishing lip aperture. The diminishing volume requires a constantly diminishing lip aperture. Therefore, these two conditions augment each other, requiring a relatively drastic change from large to small lip aperture during the course of the passage.

attention on the importance of the correct aperture size. The usual fault of students facing this playing problem is to permit the lip aperture to remain far too big in the upper register.

Our last rule pertaining to the lip aperture is related to the previous one and simply states it in reverse: A DESCENDING PASSAGE REQUIRING A *CRESCENDO* WILL NECESSITATE A DRASTIC ENLARGEMENT OF THE LIP APERTURE DURING THE DESCENT.

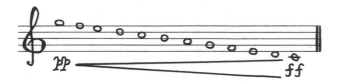

Fig. 25. The descending notes require a constantly enlarging lip aperture. The increasing volume requires a constantly enlarging lip aperture. Therefore, these two conditions augment each other, requiring a relatively drastic change from small to large lip aperture during the course of the passage.

The *conscious* application of these statements will help the student who is experiencing difficulties in producing a clear, focused tone in all registers. The lip aperture and the air column must be a "matched set" for any note at any volume. The sooner the student can combine these two elements correctly and consciously, the sooner they can enter the subconscious mind, where they must be when a difficult passage requires him to pay attention to several things at the same time!

Methods of Changing Lip Aperture Size

Earlier we have given much attention to how the correctly *shaped* lip aperture is formed, and we have emphasized the importance of the correct *size* of this opening. Now, the various ways we accomplish this *changing size* will be discussed. First, remember that the opening must change in *size* for the various ranges in pitch and volume, but it must not change in *shape*. The simplest embouchure action that will achieve this goal is the contraction of the orbicularis oris (see Fig. 9, page 13), the circle of muscle around the mouth. If we consider our "coffee can and cloth bag" analogy again, we can better visualize why the contraction of this circle of muscle is so important to maintaining this "oboe reed" shape. As we pull the drawstring of the bag tighter and tighter, the opening becomes smaller and smaller, but *always* retains its circular shape. But if we were to try to make this opening progressively smaller by pulling the opening sideways from each side, as the cheeks would do in the smiling embouchure method of obtaining high notes, the opening would get flatter and flatter in its up-down di-

mension, and longer and longer in its side-to-side dimension. These are exactly the two conditions that we do *not* want—a longer vibrating arc on the higher notes, and a constantly changing aperture shape. Of course, as it is an "oboe reed" shape that we desire and not a circular opening, the cheek muscles *do* contract to pull this opening sideways from each side. But it is the contraction of the circle of muscle around the mouth which prevents the cheeks from *completely* flattening and stretching the aperture. In visualizing this action of the cheek muscles as they oppose the mouth orifice muscles, we can understand how wrong it is for the misinformed student to stretch his lip corners farther and farther apart as he attempts to go higher in range.

To sum up this idea, the cheek muscles must try to pull the lip corners into a smile, but the circle of muscle around the lips must contract and try to prevent this smile from taking place. The cheek muscles and all the other muscles which radiate out from the orbicularis oris, and their opposition to this muscle, have been described in detail several times in the course of this book. This reiteration is permissible, I believe, because of the extreme importance of the action involved. Earlier, this idea was stressed to enable us to produce that resilient, vibratory quality so important to producing a good sound. Now we find the very same action is essential in producing a lip aperture which can vary in size while maintaining its similarity of shape.

Another aspect of brass playing which has a direct bearing on forming and maintaining the lip aperture in that important oboe-reed shape is the consideration of how far apart the upper and lower front teeth are held. It is perfectly possible to have the jaw properly thrust forward, as emphasized earlier, and yet have the teeth clenched too closely together, or for that matter, held too far apart. It has been my experience that the more usual fault lies in keeping the teeth too close together. As an experiment, lower the jaw from a clenched position (lips together and jaw forward, nevertheless) until the front teeth are separated by a quarter-inch or more. As the jaw is lowered you can actually feel the lips "thin out" slightly and come inward a bit toward the teeth, helping achieve that "lips perpendicular to the air-stream" position. Now buzz the rim, and while observing in the mirror, slowly clench and unclench the teeth while holding the jaw in its correct forward position. Note that as the jaw lowers, the little lip aperture opens up and becomes less flat. As the usual cause of a small, hard tone is too flat an aperture, it can readily be understood how playing with a slightly more lowered jaw will influence this aperture advantageously.

Next play on the instrument itself. Hold a long tone in a comfortable register, at the same time lowering and raising the jaw rhythmically two or three times a second. This will result in a jaw-vibrato very similar to that used by jazz reed players. Gradually slow this jaw-vibrato down to a speed sufficiently slow to permit critical analysis of the tone quality. Notice how, as the jaw goes up, the tone gets thick and choked, while as it gets to its lowest point, the tone becomes hollow, un-centered, and usually flat in pitch. Now continue this slow "jawing" motion (perhaps another breath will be needed by this time) and slowly reduce the *amount* of jaw motion, both in the upward and the downward direction. The object of this gradual reduction of motion is to arrive and finally stop at the most well-focused, free, big, beautiful tone that one can produce. When the jaw motion finally focuses and stops at the most satisfying sound, most of us will find, to our surprise, that the jaw, in order to achieve this best possible tone, has halted in a comparatively open position. That is, we find the upper and lower front teeth held farther apart than we had assumed was necessary. Yet, if this is the jaw position which achieves a full, free tone, we should take note of it and learn to hold the jaw in this manner habitually.

Some players may find this idea a bit difficult to grasp. I have found it helpful to suggest to such players that they play while holding the mouth as though they were yawning while holding the lips together—a sort of suppressed yawn. Or perhaps the suggestion to hold the interior of the mouth in the same position it would assume in pronouncing the vowel "O" will convey the proper feeling. This concept of the lowered jaw and the feeling of a large "cavernous" oral cavity is very important to the heightening and arching of the lip aperture and consequently to the free production of a large, clear tone. So give it proper and respectful consideration.

We have studied in detail the various important features of the brass player's embouchure. Now, before continuing to the other phases of playing, which are also vital to the art of brass playing, study Fig. 26, on which I have labeled the main features to watch for in forming this embouchure. This photograph is typical of the expression one finds on the faces of all good brass players when they are intent on their performance and are using all the involved muscles energetically, firmly and confidently. Refer to the twelve other photographs in this book (pages 26 to 31), of brass players in action. Note the great similarity of facial expressions. It might not be true that making a similar expression will guarantee success in brass playing, but I believe it can safely be said that if one does *not* make a similar expression he will *not* be a successful brass player. With the information given thus far in this book, it should be possible to combine all the components of a successful embouchure, and, with the aid of these photographs and your own mirror, to duplicate that very important clue to the art of good brass playing, "the brass player's face".

44

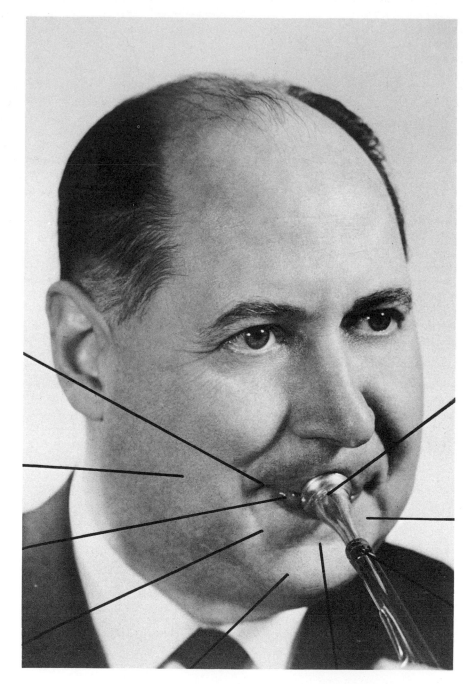

Lips are puck-
ered, cheek
muscles are
not stretching
lips.

Cheeks have
tension, as
though smiling.

Lower lip is not
tucked-in nor
swallowed be-
hind upper lip.

"U" shaped val-
ley formed by
muscle tension.

Mouthpiece
correctly
placed on the
lips in its up-
down position—
according to the
instrument be-
ing played.

Jaw is not
clenched shut,
but is held quite
open, teeth well
apart.

Instrument kept
quite horizon-
tal.

Lower jaw is
thrust forward
so that lower
front teeth align
with upper front
teeth.

Chin arched
down. No hori-
zontal wrinkle.

Fig. 26. Embouchure components which combine to form "the brass player's face."

6. Articulation

If we were to consider the tone of a brass instrument as a sort of semi-fluid building material like wet cement or clay, we might then say that it is the *tongue* which forms or molds this plastic material into building blocks or bricks. Just as any type of building can be constructed if one has sufficient sizes and shapes of bricks at his disposal, so can any musical idea be expressed if one has at his disposal notes of various lengths, pitches, and volumes.

We have only two ways to begin or articulate a note: by slurring to it from a previous note, or by starting it with an "attack" of the tongue. In two respects the tonguing of a note is the more important consideration because: 1.) The first note of a series *must* be started with the tongue; 2.) reiteration of the same note *must* be accomplished by tonguing. Even though slurring is a most important fundamental of brass playing, there are only two basic types of slur, smooth and forceful, whereas there are many types of tonguing. Therefore, let us discuss first this more complex articulation.

The Function of the Lips in Tonguing

Actually a note can be started without the help of the tongue. It can be started the same way one starts a first note while whistling—with just a gentle push of air, a sort of "ha" attack. The only trouble with such an attack is that the player cannot be quite sure just when the lips will "catch" on this air stream and start vibrating. Such uncertainty, of course, is unthinkable for the split-second timing required in the performance of music. Therefore, wind instrument players resort to various types of attacks to assure the production of the tone *exactly* when needed. So it is important for us to remember that the fundamental reason we apply the attack is *to start the lips vibrating at the exact moment they should.* Yet how often when a student attempts his attack, we hear the sound of escaping air a fraction of a second before the note "takes hold". If such a student would remember that the prime reason for the attack is to "trigger" the *lip* vibration, this very realization would result in an instinctively better attack.

The fact that the tongue simply acts to start the lip vibration in a precise manner suggests the foremost reason for poor quality tonguing. *The lips are to blame, not the tongue!* If the lips are not held so that they will vibrate exactly in sympathy with the pitch of the instrument of that moment, no amount of careful tonguing will produce clear attacks. Only the lips can influence the pitch. The tongue simply determines the starting moment of the vibration, whose pitch the *lips must have already predetermined*. True, badly focused lips can be made to start vibrating by exploding them with a *sforzando* attack, but it is just this necessity to hammer the attack which leads the unwary player to believe that there is something wrong with his tonguing. So before considering the various phases of tonguing, let us first make sure that faulty attacks are not caused by the lips, as they are in so many players. One of the tests is made by simply repeating a note, tonguing it several times in succession. If the attacks seem to become cleaner and lighter after a blurred initial attack, it simply means that the ear, the lips and the instinct begin to cooperate too late in focusing or "zeroing in" on the *exact* pitch of the note. If the same precision of pitch were applied to the very *first* note, it too would vibrate immediately and cleanly. Obviously, it is important to develop this ability to focus the lips *before* each note, particularly before the *first* note of a group.

One of the finest exercises advocated by many of the older German brass instructors is the practicing of attacks without aid from the tongue. More frequent use of this exercise would clear up many of our so-called tonguing problems. For perhaps ten minutes a day play slow scales (*andante* half-notes), starting each note with a slow, gentle push of air, using the articulation "ha". The idea is to let the air through the lips, at first without causing any sound, and then, with a quick but gentle *crescendo* of air, make the air "catch" the lips and start them vibrating *exactly* on the pitch intended. If the pitch is the least bit too high or too low, the reluctance of the instrument to start vibrating will be felt very distinctly. But when the lips learn to focus accurately on the pitch, the instrument will sound, quickly and easily, on the slightest zephyr of air. The lightest touch of the tongue would now be sufficient for a clean attack because the instrument and lips are vibrating in sympathy. In fact, it is almost impossible to produce a bad attack with even the most haphazard type of tonguing. Try it! Articulate the syllables, "Doo", "Goo", "Loo", or even "Zoo", and the instrument will still produce a very passable attack, *as long as the pitch of the lip vi-*

46

bration agrees with the pitch of the desired note on the instrument.

Another simple test of one's accuracy of pitch production is made by buzzing the mouthpiece alone. After missing an attack on the horn, take the mouthpiece off the instrument and try to buzz the note just missed. It is usually a shock to hear how far off pitch you actually were, and yet the instrument had been expected to cooperate somehow with this out-of-tune attack. Now, repeatedly attack the same note several more times on the mouthpiece alone until it can be produced with perfect intonation. Then, replace the mouthpiece on the horn and try the recalcitrant note again. This time the better result should prove to you that lip focusing is of utmost importance in obtaining clean attacks. Even though with practice it will finally be relegated to the subconscious mind, this focusing process *must* take place. When this lip buzzing accuracy-of-pitch is developed to a high degree, several improvements will take place in one's playing. In the first place, the hoped for clean attack now becomes a reality. But there are additional benefits—better intonation, better accuracy and better tone quality. The reason for these improvements is quite simple. A clean attack is caused by a lip vibration which is accurately tuned to the note desired; good intonation (provided the instrument is correctly tuned) is caused by a lip vibration which is accurately tuned to the note desired; concerning accuracy, a broken note is just a note that is *too far* out of tune; and a beautiful tone can only result from well-centered placement of pitch on each note. Thus we see the interrelationship of the various phases of brass playing and the importance which must be placed on the correctly vibrated lip. Another way of stating this relationship might be to say that progressively more inaccurate pitch production by the lips results in progressively worse stages of deterioration to any note—good attack; fuzzy attack; poor tone; bad intonation; broken note!

The cure for this inaccuracy is the regular practice of mouthpiece buzzing. Even more basic is the buzzing of the lips alone. This can be done to advantage for a few minutes a day by attempting to buzz a simple melody. Choose something with a very limited range, like "America". The lips, without the aid of the mouthpiece rim, cannot buzz very high. This is because the mouthpiece rim, as it curves around to the vertical and crosses the lips, acts like a fret on the fingerboard of a stringed instrument. The rim, where it touches the lips, stops the vibration from continuing outward beyond the mouthpiece rim. This shorter vibrating area naturally has a higher pitch. A very simple demonstration of this fact can be made by merely touching

a finger tip to each side of the center of the lips while they are buzzing. The pitch will immediately jump upward. A clue to the importance of the mouthpiece diameter can be sensed from this simple act.

Next, buzz the mouthpiece alone. You could also buzz the rim alone, but most players find this extremely difficult to do and it is doubtful whether it has any advantage over buzzing the actual mouthpiece. The object of buzzing the mouthpiece is to produce a good "rich" buzz, and one which is *exactly* in tune. With the mouthpiece alone it is possible to play just as high or low as it is while playing the instrument. In fact, *if you can't play it on the mouthpiece, you can't play it on the instrument.*

This lengthy discourse on the buzzing of the lips might seem to have been out of place in the section entitled, "Tonguing", but the proper pitch of the buzz is so closely related to successful tonguing that I cannot help but feel that this was exactly the right place for its consideration.

We can now discuss the tongue's action in the fundamental types of tonguing.

Clean, Firm Attack

As a clean, firm attack is the foundation for all attacks, let us discuss it first. The very word "attack" is misleading as it implies a forward thrust of the tongue. In rapid tonguing it seems as though the tongue *is* thrusting forward for each attack, but it is the speed of the action which causes this illusion. When we tongue slowly, we find that the tongue goes up and slightly forward *before* the attack in order to hermetically seal off the air-column and thus prevent it from continuing through the lips. The actual "attack" is the pulling away of the tip of the tongue, which breaks this hermetic seal and allows the air to suddenly start between the lips, causing them to vibrate at a precise moment. This whole procedure can be summed up by whispering very distinctly the syllable "too".

One might think of a series of tongued notes as simply a long note which is cut into separate segments by the tongue. When one thinks in this way, the logic of moving the tip of the tongue in an up-and-down direction becomes apparent. So many players have the mistaken idea that the tongue should move back-and-forth—piston-like. Suppose we use a quite homely simile. A long sausage lies horizontal on a cutting board. In order to cut it into slices, one must move the knife up and down vertically. This is exactly the function of the tongue on the air-column. Its tip must move up and down in order to cut the long horizontal air-stream into segments. The first time this is attempted, two things immediately become apparent. First, the tongue, if it is to be pulled in a downward direction, cannot be placed between the teeth, but must be placed higher in the mouth—up against the point where the upper front teeth join the gums. Second, the tip of the tongue, as it moves downward *across* the air-column during the attack, does not experience the same unpleasant resistance to the pent-up air pressure that is encountered when the tongue is pulled *backward* against the air-column, which is traveling forcefully in the opposite direction. Most of us have heard it reiterated that one must never "tongue" between the teeth. The reason now becomes apparent. Correct tonguing is an up-and-down motion, but when the tongue is placed between the teeth, the only direction it can move for the attack is backward.

Sforzando Attack

There is one type of attack which does call for the placing of the tip of the tongue between the teeth. That is the *sforzando* or heavy accent. "Bell tones" are also in this category. Here an audible explosion is actually desirable and the forceful breaking of the hermetic seal immediately back of the lips is most effectively achieved by the sudden backward pull of the tongue against the pent-up air.

But this type of attack must be considered unusual, and the normal, moderate type of attack is still best achieved by pulling the tongue *downward* from a point near the gumline of the upper front teeth.

Legato Attack

A softer-than-normal attack is used to articulate very smooth, *legato* passages. Again the up-down direction of the tip of the tongue is maintained, but now the syllable "doo" is whispered instead of "too" (I suggest that it be whispered, rather than voiced, because in the past I have heard students who took too literally the instruction to "*say* too" and actually activated the vocal chords!). A little experimenting will demonstrate that the syllable "doo" can be enunciated with the tip of the tongue in exactly the same spot behind the teeth as it was for the syllable "too". The difference is in the suddenness with which the tongue is moved. For the "too" sound, the tip was pulled down fast and rather forcibly; at the same time, the air pressure was applied with enough force to produce the desired amount of mild "explosion". But for the "doo" attack, the tongue tip is pulled away more slowly and gently, and with less pent-up pressure behind it. This downward stroke is so gentle that it feels as though

the tongue were being "peeled" away by an undulating motion which breaks the hermetic seal so quietly that there is no perceptible explosion. The air simply starts cleanly and definitely, but without accent. This *legato* tonguing is a most important factor in playing a beautiful, singing, melodic line and should be practiced very conscientiously.

Staccato Tonguing

A discussion on articulation would not be complete without a thorough description of *staccato* tonguing. But first, let me define *staccato*. A *staccato* note is a short note. A *staccato* passage is one in which the notes are separated from each other by periods of silence. *Staccato* does *not* mean as short as possible, but only relatively shorter than the normal value of the note. There are many passages in Beethoven's music, for example, where we find a *staccato* mark (a dot) over half-notes in a slow passage. These notes are simply separated from each other by short rests, so that they are approximately dotted quarters followed by eighth rests. Some music dictionaries define a *staccato* note as one held approximately half its original value. From these definitions it should be clear that the determining factor in producing a true *staccato* is how the note is *released*, not how it is *attacked*. True, a well-tongued *staccato* note must be separated from its neighbors on *both* sides, not only by its release, but also by the clarity of its attack. But to claim that the clarity with which a note is tongued determines whether it will be *staccato* or not is to imply that a *sostenuto* note need *not* be tongued clearly. This is ridiculous, of course, as a long note is entitled to just as clean a start as any other note.

Therefore, when we consider the difficulties of producing a good *staccato*, we should be mainly concerned with the production of *very short notes*. The importance of the well-focused lips in successful, clean attacks has already been stressed and applies equally to long and short notes. But the release of a very short note, coming, as it does, right on the heels of the attack, is most often the point of technical failure. Too often the misguided player attempts to get shortness in his *staccato* notes by stopping the vibration with the tongue—"tut tut tut". This abrupt stopping of the air-column, and its consequent abrupt stoppage of the tone, produces a most unmusical and unnatural quality. No *musical* instrument in the world stops its sound suddenly. All of them, including xylophone and *pizzicato* violin, invariably produce tones with tapered endings. In other words, any *musical* note, no matter how short, has a *diminuendo* at its very end which tapers it down to inaudibility. In extremely short notes, this effect takes place so rapidly that it is almost impossible to analyze—but take place it must! So we see that stopping a note with the tongue by the use of some syllable such as "tut" or "toot", while it might achieve extreme shortness, will never be musically effective. All notes properly played on a brass instrument, long or short, have a tapered ending. I do not mean to imply that all notes should have a *diminuendo*. The taper to which I refer occurs only at the last fraction of a second and would take place on a long "straight" note which required no *diminuendo*, and even on a *crescendo* note. Here is a little diagram (Fig. 27) which will illustrate this idea graphically:

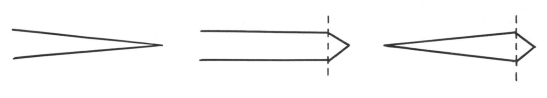

Fig. 27   Ordinary *diminuendo*   Straight tone   Ordinary *crescendo*

This *diminuendo* effect often occurs only in the last fraction of a second, but the result gives the effect that the notes "ring" or are left hanging in the air. In fact, notes played in this manner can make even the dullest room sound resonant. Now, although we want this "ring" even on our shortest *staccato* notes, it must be accomplished in a very short span of time, or else the note will lose its *staccato* quality.

Instead of enunciating "tut", which stops a note dead, or "too", which might allow it to ring *too* long, try the enunciation "tuh". This achieves a very short note, but does not permit the tongue to go back up into its preparatory position, where it would forcibly stop the air flow. The "uh" of the "tuh" articulation successfully stops the air-column short, but allows a little tail-end wisp of air to follow through the lip aperture. This creates that tiny *diminuendo* so necessary for a live, ringing quality in even the shortest *staccato*.

Beside the "tut", method, there is one other inartistic way to obtain a very short note. It is seldom attempted, but I have observed it just often enough in students to feel the need to give warning. This is the method of obtaining a short *staccato* by forcibly stopping the air-column with the articulation "tup". Because he is not resorting to stopping the air with the tongue as in "tut", the player believes that he is proceeding correctly. But, enunciating "tup" closes the lip aperture at the end of the note and produces almost exactly the same abrupt, unmusical effect that resulted from the articulation "tut". The conscientious formation of the syllable "tuh" and the preservation of the correctly shaped lip opening (even after the note has ended!) will correct this extremely bad habit.

One of the fundamental problems of brass playing is the rapid tonguing of a series of notes. Some players can "single-tongue" notes much more rapidly than other players, and, inasmuch as we all have approximately the same physical equipment, this ability must be attributed to their more efficient use of their equipment. Here are four aids which will contribute to light, rapid tonguing.

1. The lips, as stressed before, must be focused very carefully and precisely on the pitch desired, if the instrument is to "speak" lightly and instantaneously.

2. The tongue should work in an up-and-down direction from a position back of the upper front teeth and not in-and-out between the teeth. This speeds up the tongue, because it is working *across* the direction of the air pressure, and not *with* it in one direction and *against* it in the other.

3. The stroke of the tongue should be made very short. The larger the tongue's motion, the longer the round-trip takes. Note the size of the bore of the mouthpiece, or better yet, the general size of the lip aperture. There is no good reason why the tongue, when it pulls down to initiate an attack, should form an air-passage larger than the lip aperture or the mouthpiece bore. The smallest of these apertures will determine how much air can get through the instrument, in any case. Even when the tongue is pulled down as little as a sixteenth of an inch, the area of the resultant horizontal slot between the tongue and the upper gums will far exceed the area of the mouthpiece bore or the lip aperture. There-

fore, in the interest of speed, the brass player should practice tonguing with as little motion as possible. When done correctly, the main body of the tongue remains motionless, while only the tip flicks up and down for as short a distance as is consistent with the volume of sound (and consequently air) desired.

4. For the first note of a rapidly tongued passage, we usually need a crisp, clean attack, and so we use the syllable "tuh". But the following notes, coming in rapid succession, can be played much faster and lighter if the hermetic seal is not made too tight. Making and breaking a perfectly tight hermetic seal between the tip of the tongue and the gum-line of the upper front teeth is both time-consuming and fatiguing. It requires time to create a perfect seal and effort to break it open for each note. Therefore, after the initial note, use the syllable "duh", or even the syllable "thuh" (sounded as in "though" and *not* as in "thud"). A rapidly tongued passage would then be articulated in this way: "Tuh-duh-duh-duh-duh", or "Tuh-thuh-thuh-thuh-thuh".

To sum up these four aids briefly: 1.) focus the lip "buzz" accurately on the desired pitch, 2.) move only the tip of the tongue, and only in an up-and-down direction, 3.) make the stroke of the tongue as short as possible, and, 4.) do not create a tight hermetic seal, but let the tongue touch lightly—almost to the point of letting air escape between notes.

These four aids will do wonders for increasing the speed of the tongue, but only when combined and used in complete synchronization. This, of course, will only be achieved with practice, and the metronome is our best practice aid. Start with a *tempo* on the metronome which is slow enough to permit easy execution of the passage, even while employing the four new aids. Then advance the metronome speed notch by notch and *day by day*. This will result in controlled advancement that can, in a few weeks or months, improve any player's single-tonguing speed to the point of handling most fast passages.

Double- and Triple-Tonguing

When a tongued passage occurs which is too fast to be single-tongued, the brass player can always resort to double- or triple-tonguing. I use the word "resort" purposely because, in my opinion, these two types of tonguing should only be used as a last resort. Not that there is anything wrong or cowardly about their use, but there is a tendency for brass players, as they become proficient in double- and triple-tonguing, to use them more and more frequently, even on passages slow enough to be single-tongued. This ultimately results in a single-tongue which becomes sluggish simply through disuse. So develop an efficient double- and triple-tongue, but, at the same time, resolve only to use them when the *tempo* absolutely cannot be handled by single-tonguing.

As the double- and triple-tonguing principles are similar, I will first describe the procedure for double-tonguing, because of its less complex nature. Even the fastest single-tongue requires time to "reset" its position for the next attack, and the amount of time determines the speed of the tonguing. The principle involved in double-tonguing is to attack, by some other means, another note between the normal "too" attacks, actually producing this note while the tip of the tongue is "resetting" for its next attack. The method used to obtain this intermediate attack is the pronunciation of the consonant "K". A series of double-tongued notes might then be articulated "too-koo-too-koo-too-koo". However, as the "K" attack is made by the back of the tongue against the roof of the mouth just forward of the soft palate, the tongue can be put into better position for double-tonguing by using another *vowel*. By enunciating "tih" and "kih", the back of the tongue is arched up into much better striking distance of the roof of the mouth. With this modification a practical articulation for double-tonguing becomes "tih-kih-tih-kih-tih-kih". This principle can be easily grasped by reversing the syllables and saying rapidly a phrase we have all used at some time, "(Here) kitty-kitty-kitty-kitty." If you can say this rapidly, you can double-tongue, as once the phrase is started, it is immaterial which syllable (tih or kih) started the series, as they follow each other alternately in either case.

A further refinement of double-tonguing articulation can be used when the passage requires extremely fast and light articulation. Here we again apply the principle offered earlier to aid fast single-tonguing—the avoidance of a complete "hermetic seal" by the tongue. You remember, that to avoid this sealing of the air-column, we used the articulation "doo" or "dih", rather than "too" or "tih". In exactly the same way we lighten our double-tonguing by using the syllable "dih" for the first note of the double-tongue, and avoid the hermetic seal caused by the "K" sound by substituting the consonant, "G", as sounded in the word "Good". Thus our articulation for extremely light, fast double-tonguing becomes "dih-gih-dih-gih-dih-gih".

When double-tonguing is first applied to a brass

instrument, it is found to be more difficult to *play* the syllables than to *say* them. This results from the fact that when playing on the instrument, the tongue is working in a field of compressed-air, which gives it a heavy, logy feeling. There is an even more basic reason why one's first attempts at double-tonguing produce such disconcertingly bad results. The syllable "tih" is articulated well forward in the mouth, so that the tiny explosion takes place close enough to the mouthpiece to give the attack the desired, clean, sudden start. But the syllable "kih", starting a great deal farther back in the mouth, has a much bigger cushion of air between its point of origin and the mouthpiece than did the syllable "tih". This cushion of air gives a softening effect to the attack so that the "kih" tends to sound much less firm than the "tih". In order to prevent this, the "K" sound has to be "kicked" very hard. The feeling is as though the "kih" is articulated harder and louder than the "tih". Of course, the ear must be checking the result constantly, and dictating to the tongue, lips and breath what must be done to achieve the most even single-tongue effect possible. One exercise which is very helpful in learning to strengthen the "K" part of double-tonguing is to reverse the syllables occasionally—"kih-tih-kih-tih". This puts the "K's" on the emphatic notes of the passage, forcibly calling attention to their inherent weakness. If they can now be "kicked" hard enough to make the series of notes convincingly even, the biggest difficulty in double- *and* triple-tonguing will have been solved. Although we must emphasize this hard "K" sound while learning to double-tongue, we can relax this hardness when refining the process into "dih-gih-dih-gih-dih-gih", simply because when the "tih" is softened to "dih" we can then afford to soften the "kih" to "gih" to maintain a matched set of articulations.

Strangely enough, many students, when first studying double-tonguing, can attain great speed, although it is usually quite uncontrolled. So it is essential when learning both double- and triple-tonguing to play very slowly and evenly. The unevenness, so difficult to prevent, is much more pronounced at a slow speed and can thus be corrected more satisfactorily. Then, as the speed is gradually increased, the evenness will be easily maintained.

Although fast double- and triple-tonguing is desirable (and seemingly never neglected by the average player!), the practice of these two types of tonguing at a relatively slow, *controlled tempo* is far too often overlooked. Imagine the incongruity of a player who can single-tongue sixteenth notes up to a speed of ♩=120 on the metronome, and yet can double-tongue sixteenths no *slower* than ♩=144. He

has a large *tempo* range between ♩=120 and ♩=144 in which he has no means of tonguing! There are too many of this type player. How much more intelligent it would be to improve one's single-tonguing up to a speed of ♩=126 or 132 and improve one's double-tonguing *down* to ♩=120. Then there would be an overlap of abilities which would enable the player to negotiate all tongued passages from the slowest to the fastest.

As in double-tonguing, the principle of triple-tonguing is based on the premise that resetting the tip of the tongue takes time—too much time for some passages—and this resultant wait should be filled in by some other means of articulation. This "other means" in both double- and triple-tonguing is the quite forcible pronunciation of the syllable "kih". Triple-tonguing, as its name implies, is employed in the articulation of triplets, or multiples of triplets. As there are only two basic ways of tonguing, the "T" attack and the "K" attack, it stands to reason that one of these must be articulated twice in order to produce a group of three notes. Although the tongue finds it difficult to repeat "T-T-T-T-T" at a very high speed, it can enunciate two "T's" in a row quite rapidly. Then, just when the tongue would start to get sluggish on the third note, the syllable "K" is substituted, while the tip of the tongue resets for another group of two "T's". Combined with the "ih" vowel, for the correctly arched tongue, a series of triple-tongued notes then appears like this: "tih-tih-kih-tih-tih-kih-tih-tih-kih". The very rapid, light version of this tonguing will be articulated like this: "dih-dih-gih-dih-dih-gih-dih-dih-gih". As in double-tonguing, this articulation must be practiced slowly and evenly, and the speed increased only as control is gained.

Occasionally, brass players get into heated discussions with flute players, who contend that the proper articulation for triple-tonguing is "tih-kih-tih-tih-kih-tih-tih-kih-tih", with the "K" attack in the middle of each group of three. But this is splitting hairs, for a glance at the figure will show that this series, once started, continues to repeat two "T's" and one "K" just as the brass players' articulation does.

When using double- and triple-tonguing in actual passage work, it often happens that the passage does not start out with a complete unit, but only part of a group, and this often requires the tonguing to commence with the "K" articulation. This is good form—the only correct way to get these passages to "come out even". Following are a few examples of groups of double- and triple-tongued notes which commence with a partial group.

In double-tongued passages, the decision to start with "T" or "K" is quite simple. If it starts "offbeat" with an odd number of "pick-up notes", it starts with "K". All even numbered groups start with "T". See Fig. 28.

Fig. 28

In triple-tonguing, when the passage begins with the last two notes of a triplet group, these two notes are tongued "T-K", as in double-tonguing. If the passage begins with only the last note of a triplet group, this note is tongued "K". See Fig. 29.

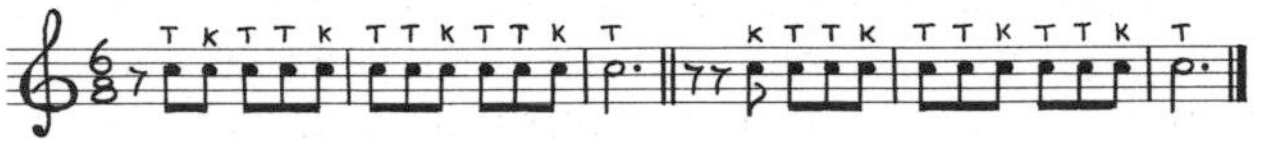

Fig. 29

Many ingenious combinations of double- and triple-tonguing can be employed along with the choice of whether to start with the "T" or "K". These are so varied and so much a matter of individual preference that little more can be said about them other than to urge experimentation. For example, many players will solve certain triplet passages with double-tonguing, emphasizing the proper notes regardless of whether they occur on the "T" or the "K". See Fig. 30. The combination possibilities are limited only by the individual player's imagination and control of single-, double- and triple-tonguing.

Fig. 30

For the study of tonguing, nothing is likely to surpass the famous and readily available *Arban Method*. This is printed by several publishers and can be obtained in either treble or bass clef, making it practical for all the brass instruments. In it will be found an extensive and well-paced section devoted to triple-tonguing and another devoted to double-tonguing. Although, in his book, Arban advocates the study of triple-tonguing first and double-tonguing later, I have had more success with my own pupils by reversing the procedure and teaching the simpler

(in my estimation) double-tonguing first. My procedure for the practice of both double- and triple-tonguing is as follows. Each exercise is played through four times, and, as they are short, several can be practiced each day. First, the exercise is played as rapidly as possible *single-tongued*. The second time it is played at *exactly* the same speed, but this time double- (or triple-) tongued. The third time it is double- or triple-tongued as fast as it can be played *evenly* and *cleanly*. The fourth time it is played absolutely as fast as possible, even to the point where control is lost. This last reckless *tempo* is needed to improve the day-by-day speed. With the aid of a metronome, the speed of the double- and triple-tonguing, as well as the speed of the single-tonguing, can, day-by-day, be pushed imperceptibly, but steadily, forward. Remember that correct methods are essential to fast, effortless tonguing, but even these methods require daily, conscientious practice in order to produce satisfying results.

Slurs and Legato Playing

As stated earlier, there are only two ways a note can be started on a brass instrument--either by an attack of the tongue, or by being slurred into from a previous note of different pitch. Notice that there are two important limitations to a slur: It cannot start the first note of a passage and it cannot be used to reiterate notes of the same pitch.

In explanation of the above title, we usually think of a slur as a smooth slide between two notes of different pitch, accomplished without aid from the tongue. A *legato* passage consists of all, or nearly all, slurred notes. Therefore, if we understand the mechanics of a good slur between *two* notes, we automatically know the correct way to play *complete legato passages*.

The first important clue to good slurring is found in the foregoing statement that the *first note* of a series must be tongued. The moment the lips cease to vibrate, a *legato* series, by definition, has ended. Whether this occurs purposely or accidentally is beside the point. Yet the biggest mistake made by players with poor slurs is in permitting the lip vibration to *cease* between notes. The moment this happens, there is no practical way (one might even say, no *legal* way!) to commence the next note except with an attack of the tongue. Therefore, the first rule for a good *legato* is basic and simple: do not allow the lips to stop vibrating *between* notes. The buzz itself will have no particular pitch while in this "no-man's land" between notes, as it is in rapid transition, pitch-wise. But when the pitch reaches the desired note and centers itself at that point, the instrument will automatically speak, as the lips are already in vibration, *never having stopped vibrating*.

The feeling is that the buzzing lips make a rapid *glissando* from one note to the next. This is precisely what they do, but the *glissando* must be rapid and must stop accurately upon the desired pitch, or other intervening notes of the same fingering will be "picked up" along the way, spoiling the *legato* quality of the slur.

It should be quite obvious that a well-supported air-column must *continue between* the notes to keep this buzz alive. So many players have a misconception that the air-column "bulges" on each note and continues only as a mere thread of air between these notes—a sort of hourglass effect rather than a straight column. The air-column must continue straight and steady between notes with just as much support from the diaphragm as would be used to sustain one long tone.

Vowel Sounds as an Aid to Slurring

In spite of the need for a steady stream of air, a *little* push of air would help secure the notes in an upward slur, as would a moderate relaxing of the air-pressure aid in a downward slur. But to attempt to get this aid by shoving or relaxing the air-column through the use of the diaphragm would be much too crude for smooth *legato* results. Most brass players use a method of obtaining this desired light push without forcing with the diaphragm. This consists of the subtle use of the vowel sounds "oh", "ah" and "ee". There is a natural (and, in my opinion, quite correct) tendency to form the inside of the mouth for the vowel "oh", while holding low notes, "ah" or "oo" for the middle register, and "ee" for the high register. These vowel sounds do not change from one to another at any certain point in the range, but rather change imperceptibly and gradually as the range ascends or descends. That is, the "oh" formation of the lower notes *gradually* becomes "ee" in the high register by the *gradual* arching higher and higher of the back of the tongue. This process works in reverse as the player descends.

In slurring very small intervals, this action is almost imperceptible. But, in the slurring of larger intervals, this change becomes quite pronounced. For example, in the upward slur of an octave, one could very advantageously form the vowel "oh" for the lower note and, while the lip buzz is making a rapid *glissando* upward, arch the tongue to form the vowel "ee" on the upper note. Thus, two actions synchronize on this upward slur. The lip buzz makes a continuous unbroken upward *glissando* and the tongue makes the vowel transition, "oh-ee". For a down-

ward slur the process is reversed, the pitch of the lip buzz making a *glissando* downward, while the vowel transition becomes "ee-oh".

By the use of these various vowels, we add two subtle aids to our playing finesse: 1.) We furnish that desired *gentle* push on upward slurs and the *gentle* easing of air-pressure on downward slurs. This occurs because the changing of the vowel by the arching or lowering of the tongue changes the air capacity of the mouth cavity. The upward arching of the back of the tongue sends a minute quantity of air already in the oral cavity along with the steadily moving air-column, reinforcing it with just the desired additional impetus. The beauty of this method is in the delicacy with which it can be applied and the subtlety of the result. The lowering of the arched tongue from "ee" to "ah" on a large downward slur enlarges the oral cavity. This, in turn, gently reduces the air-pressure just at the moment when it is most desirable to do so. As the lip aperture suddenly becomes larger at the bottom of a downward slur, this reduction of air-pressure is very much needed to prevent the lower note from blurting out unmusically. 2.) The formation of vowels aids in the *automatic* positioning of the lips for the best production of both high and low notes. The forming of the vowel "oh" or "ah" for the lower notes requires the jaw to be lowered, which in turn tends to open the lips. As the lip aperture must be larger for the low notes anyway, this is a most happy circumstance. Conversely, the "ee" position formed by the tongue and interior of the mouth for the higher notes influences the lower jaw to rise *slightly*, and the lips automatically come into better position for the small aperture required.

In summary, four basic procedures should help the brass player achieve that beautiful liquid *legato* so characteristic of the finest artists.

1. Keep the lips buzzing *between* the slurred notes.
2. Carefully time the up or down *glissando* buzz so that the slurs are smooth. If the *glissando* is made too slowly, intervening notes will have time to sound, spoiling the *legato*. If made too fast, slurs will be dry and hard.
3. Support the continuous buzz with a steady air-column, one which does not sag or weaken between the slurred notes.
4. By the subtle use of vowel formations in the oral cavity, aid upward slurs with "oh-ee" and downward slurs with "ee-oh".

Practice combining and synchronizing these four procedures, remembering that *legato* playing is *totally* successful only when each *individual* slur is successful.

7. Mouthpiece Pressure

Sooner or later every brass player asks himself, or *should* ask himself, "Do I use too much mouthpiece pressure?" If the answer is "yes", the next question must be, "How do I get rid of this undesirable pressure?" If we understand *why* we feel the need, at times, for undue pressure, perhaps the answer to this last question will be found more easily.

Common Pressure Problems

No one ever complains of mouthpiece pressure increasing as he descends into the low register. He may actually use too much pressure in the middle register, but it is usually only when he starts ascending into the high register that the pressure becomes intense enough to cause concern. Therefore, we can consider mouthpiece pressure a problem associated with the high register. A high note requires an extremely small aperture between the lips. This aperture can be achieved correctly only with an embouchure which is used correctly and which is in top physical condition as a result of sufficient practice. Note that an incorrectly formed embouchure will not produce easy high notes with *any* amount of practice, nor will a correctly formed embouchure produce easy high notes with *insufficient* practice. This is because these necessarily tiny apertures must not only be correct as to shape and size, but must also be resilient and vibratory. Flabby muscles will not permit easy high notes on even the most correctly formed embouchure. There is, *unfortunately,* one simple way of overcoming both the lack of the small aperture and the flabby muscles. This is through the use of mouthpiece pressure. It is such an easy thing to apply a little more of this pressure as we go higher that nearly all beginners use it instinctively and most professionals resort to it in emergencies. Yet it is extremely detrimental to good brass playing, and the regular use of excessive pressure will not only result in poor tone and sluggish technique, but will shorten the player's endurance, and, in the long run, shorten his playing years.

Through another of our homely illustrations we can visualize how heavy pressure achieves both the small aperture and the firm flesh. Imagine a nice, fresh, spongy doughnut, sandwiched between two pieces of plate-glass. If these pieces of glass are slowly pressed together, the hole in the doughnut can be observed to gradually get smaller as the doughnut itself is flattened. But, at the same time, this pressure also compresses the "flesh" of the doughnut into something much firmer than its original spongy consistency. In just this same way, mouthpiece pressure diminishes the size of the opening in the lips, while simultaneously compressing the soft flesh into something resembling strong, firm muscle. Unfortunately, the poor lips suffer the same abuse as did the crushed doughnut, and, of course, human lips cannot take this punishment indefinitely.

The understanding of why we are all occasionally tempted to use undue mouthpiece pressure and the knowledge that it *does* temporarily, but brutally, help to obtain high notes will make us better prepared to resist this temptation. There *are* ways in which we can correctly aid the production of high notes without resorting to *undue* pressure. Note that I have always referred to this pressure as *undue* pressure. This modifying word is necessary because some small amount of mouthpiece pressure is always present, and is quite harmless. There should be a comfortable, normal pressure which hermetically seals the lips to the mouthpiece—a pressure which keeps the mouthpiece from skidding around on the lips and gives a general feeling of security.

This normal pressure will vary in several ways. It will differ between individual players; it will differ on various type mouthpieces; normally, it will increase as the player goes into the higher register; it will increase as a player becomes fatigued. One of our finest trumpet players, when asked, "How much pressure do you use?" always replies, "Which end of the concert are you talking about?" But, in spite of all these variations, *normal* pressure is never so heavy as to cause deep indentations in the lips. Certainly it never cuts them or loosens the front teeth, as does *undue* pressure! This undue pressure is rather difficult to define, as there is a rather narrow line of demarcation between fairly heavy, but acceptable, pressure, and that embouchure-destroying pressure about which I warn. It is conceivable that a player habitually using excessive pressure might actually use less pressure when he is *fresh* than would a normal player when very *fatigued*. But these varying pressures are relative to many things beside the fatigue element, and our object is to help relieve pressure, even if only to a small degree, for those players who even *suspect* that they are using too much. Though there may be no exact measurement by which we can compare relative pressures, everyone has a pretty good suspicion of whether or not he needs to improve this aspect of his playing.

As previously mentioned, mouthpiece pressure is a substitute method used to fulfill two important requirements in the attainment of high notes: extremely small lip apertures and very firm flesh. Therefore, if we can gain these two requisites by more scientific and less violent means, we ought to automatically reduce pressure.

One of the reasons correct embouchure formation has been so carefully stressed is because of its importance to the player in successfully bringing the lip aperture down to a fine, clean opening—sometimes no more than a needle-hole in size. If the lower lip should slip behind the upper lip, there is an overlapping effect which will never permit this very tiny opening to exist. But, if one thrusts out the lower jaw to the right degree, the lower teeth will adequately support the lower lip, preventing this overlap. *Then* the drawstring of muscle around the mouth can draw these properly abutted lips around an extremely fine opening. At the same time, this jaw-thrust distributes more pressure onto the often neglected lower lip. Too frequently the upper lip bears the brunt of this undue pressure, and the mere act of equalizing the pressure between the upper and lower lip by the jaw-thrust does wonders for endurance, even though the *total amount* of pressure might still be too great.

The foregoing discussion shows how the one action--thrusting the lower jaw forward—serves *two* purposes: positioning the lips for production of a small lip aperture *and* equalizing the pressure on the two lips. It also illustrates well the interplay and chain-reaction of the various embouchure functions, which sometimes confuse us as to the exact cause of our trouble. It will benefit the player suffering from excessive pressure to reread the pages concerning proper embouchure, because the proper formation of the embouchure is the only correct way to achieve small apertures, and they, in turn, are a necessity for the production of high notes.

It is quite possible to play with a perfectly formed embouchure and still fail to produce good high notes. Every fine brass player is familiar with this fact. After a few days away from his instrument, he can no longer easily reach his high notes, in spite of forming his usual correct embouchure. He can get them temporarily if he resorts to pressure, but he is usually too smart a player to do that and will prefer to rebuild his embouchure muscles slowly and completely before attempting any strenuous

playing. This loss of high register through lack of practice, even for the expert, bears out the earlier statement that firm, resilient lip muscles are an indispensible requirement for the production of high notes. If this firmness is lacking because of insufficient practice, it must be furnished *artificially* by applying enough pressure to compress the flabby lips into a semblance of firmness. This pressure must also be applied when a player, in good condition, becomes fatigued near the end of a heavy playing session. In this case, however, the pressure is needed, not because of a neglected embouchure, but because fatigued muscles lose their ability to contract firmly.

Thus we see that it is the height of foolishness to decide that the embouchure is at fault in the poor production of high notes *unless* the player has first put in several hours a day of diligent practice for at least a couple of weeks before reaching this conclusion. For if the embouchure is soft, it might not be its *formation* which is causing the trouble, but only its *flabby condition*. Therefore, before making any hasty embouchure changes to improve high notes, eliminate this possibility by a week or two of conscientious practice, particularly in the high register. Even unsuccessful attempts to reach these high notes are strengthening, and perseverance often results in ultimate success. Only if no progress results should one attempt to revise the formation of the embouchure along more approved lines.

Finally, in conquering excess pressure, we must remember that it is a gradual process and will not occur as a revolutionary, overnight miracle. For the person using too much pressure is involved in a vicious downward spiral. The more pressure he uses, the less the lips will develop—the less the lips develop, the more pressure he must use. Turning this spiral upward is a subtle step, one which the player, at first, may not even believe is effective. It is begun by attempting to play with just the *slightest* bit less pressure, perhaps a decrease of only an ounce or two. *Any* brass player can apply a little less pressure than he presently uses if he consciously exhorts himself to try. The trick is to *insist* upon this almost unnoticeable decrease of pressure for several days. During this time, the lips, in an attempt to uphold the playing ability without the help of pressure, develop additional strength from their new efforts to contract more firmly. This new strength enables the pressure to be further decreased, which in turn requires the lips to become even stronger. The process continues its upward spiral until one day the player realizes that he is now playing with substantially less pressure. These little "one-ounce" improvements finally total up to an impressive difference in the amount of pressure needed. However, the process cannot be hurried, as the pressure will not be eased faster than the lips can increase their strength. This might take weeks or months, depending on one's diligence and desire to succeed. Of course, this encouraging upward spiral will not continue forever, and somewhere in that vague region which we call "normal pressure", the process will come to a halt. The player will be fully aware that even though he may still be using a moderate amount of pressure, it is far different from the brutal pressure which formerly crushed the tone, range and endurance out of his lips.

Some schools of brass-playing contend that the amount of pressure needed can gradually be reduced to zero. In fact, I have seen rather impressive demonstrations of this no-pressure theory, the player hanging a trumpet by a thread attached to the second valve key and blowing a few tones. Even though it displays a remarkable development and sense of control, I have never heard a big, beautiful, ringing tone produced with this no-pressure system. Furthermore, when the demonstrator is asked to play with a big tone, he will immediately apply the same moderate pressure which we all need, not only to seal our lips hermetically to the mouthpiece, but also to give us a sense of security and "contact" with the instrument. Even the most avid no-pressure advocate will have to start applying some pressure as his lips become fatigued.

The whole object in solving this problem of pressure is to reduce it, through lip development, to the minimum amount conducive to the desired result. When this desired result is to continue playing when very tired, undoubtedly more pressure will be required. When the desire is to play extremely high notes, heavier pressure will again be needed.

In a brief summary we can say this about mouthpiece pressure:

1.) Most of us, by exercising a bit of self-control, can advantageously reduce our general pressure, at first to only a slight degree, but later to a very substantial degree. This development takes place gradually. The constant *striving* to avoid pressure builds lip strength, lip strength in turn enables one to use less pressure.

2.) By observing correct embouchure principles, we enable the lips to align with each other properly, which not only equalizes the pressure on both lips, but also permits the lips to produce the small aperture so necessary to high notes. If a faulty embouchure prevents

this small aperture from forming, the only recourse is our old enemy, pressure.

3.) Practice is the only physical exercise which will keep the lips firm and resilient. When this firmness is absent we can only substitute pressure. So practice!

4.) Unfortunately, there are times when we will need to use heavy pressure. When these moments occur, keep in mind that pressure is for *emergency use only*, then go ahead and use it. These infrequent moments will not harm the player who conscientiously and consistently avoids pressure to the best of his ability.

Lateral Pressure

While we are on the subject of pressure, let me bring up another type of pressure often encountered, but for some reason rarely discussed or corrected. For want of a better name I will call it "lateral pressure". We usually think of pressure as a push directly in line with the mouthpiece, which exerts its force backward against the teeth with only the unfortunate lips to act as a cushion. But pressure, of course, can exert itself in any direction, and many players have a habit of pushing the mouthpiece *laterally*—at a right-angle to the direction of the mouthpipe.

This force could be to either side, or up, or down. I have observed very few players who exert this lateral pressure to either side and have found only an occasional player who forces the mouthpiece in a downward direction. But the practice of forcing the mouthpiece *upward* toward the nose can be observed in a large number of players. Usually, most of these players apply very little lateral pressure in the lower and middle registers, but apply more and more upward push as they ascend, until, in the highest register, they are exerting very noticeable amounts of this pressure. Evidence of this can be seen by the lessening distance between the top of the mouthpiece and the bottom of the nose. Usually this area directly under the nose shows a pronounced bulge, as the compressed flesh has nowhere else to go.

If players using this lateral pressure had exceptionally good high notes, we would all soon adopt the idea. However, since these players almost always have poor high registers, one wonders why they don't immediately take steps to "unadopt" this system. Perhaps there are two reasons. Some players are undoubtedly not even aware that they are using this pressure, and others cannot stop it even though they try. Then there is the unfortunate combination--the player who doesn't know he uses lateral pressure and who couldn't stop it if he did!

Although the habit can be observed occasionally in players of all the brass instruments, it seems to predominate in horn and tuba players. Possibly, this is because most horn and tuba players rest the instrument either on the leg or on the chair. Many players form a habit of tensing the neck and shoulder muscles as they go into the high register. This, plus the increase of "regular pressure", causes a player to "duck his head" slightly. Since the horn or tuba cannot give way to this force, because it is already resting on a foundation, the mouthpiece is pushed toward the nose--or more accurately, the nose is pushed toward the mouthpiece. This idea is brought up, not to excuse lateral pressure certainly, but as one possible cause for the formation of the habit, since one of the best ways to begin breaking a bad habit is to know what caused it in the first place.

There are trombonists and trumpeters who also resort to this habit, and they don't even have the excuse offered above for horn and tuba players. Perhaps they developed the habit through carelessness, or by forcing their high registers when very fatigued.

On all brass instruments there are some players who, having developed lateral pressure unconsciously, can, with plenty of hard work and determination, break the habit by simply refusing to resort to it. But there are the others who, even after they are aware of this bad habit, desire to break it and *cannot*. Here we encounter one mistake leading to another, with the neglect of one relatively simple embouchure-forming act bringing out trouble in a seemingly unrelated area. For most often, the player who is aware of, and desires to break, this upward-pressure habit has been playing with a receding jaw. This results in his holding the instrument at a downward slant. When he applies even moderate pressure for his high notes, the mouthpiece travels up the oblique angle formed between the mouthpiece and the upper front teeth, carrying the upper lip with it. The correction? Thrust the jaw forward, as suggested so often, and hold the horn at the resultant more horizontal angle so the mouthpiece is *perpendicular* to the upper front teeth.

Though I feel it a duty to mention this lateral pressure because of its frequent and detrimental use, I think it is definitely a "by-product" of some other misuse of the embouchure. When the really important components of the embouchure are employed faithfully, lateral pressure is not likely to occur.

8. Breath Control

The breath is to brass playing what the bow is to string playing. They are both motivators, setting the lips or the strings into vibration. The bow-hair is long, straight and coated with rosin. This furnishes, in effect, a long "stream of resistance" which rubs past the vibrators (strings) at right-angles. The friction of this completely controllable bow against the strings sets up any type of vibration the player wishes. A steady tone demands a steadily moving bow; a loud tone requires the bow to be moved more heavily and swiftly; short notes require the use of short segments of bow, and so on.

The parallels between bowing and the brass player's breath control are quite obvious. The air-column is released in a continuous long stream which rubs the vibrators (lips) at right-angles. A steady tone requires steadiness of the air-column; a loud tone requires a faster moving and larger air-stream; short notes require the air-stream to be cut into short segments by the tongue. These parallels have been brought out by many teachers, and I reiterate them because they help to illustrate the correct way to use the breath in playing a wind instrument.

When a string student is told to draw a bigger tone, he automatically does something definite about it with his *right* arm. He does not try to enlarge his tone with his *left* hand by using more *vibrato* or finger pressure. Because he can *see* what he is doing, the incongruity of trying to draw a big tone with his left hand never even occurs to him. Yet, because we brass players deal with less visible, or at least less tangible playing forces, just such an incongruity is often attempted by brass students. If the air-stream, as the motivator of vibration, can be compared to the violin bow, the embouchure, being the vibrator, is comparable to the violin string. In spite of this logic, how often we observe the unthinking brass student trying to evoke a bigger tone from his instrument by strenuously tensing his embouchure, or otherwise distorting it. He may try with all his might to *form* a big tone with his embouchure, but will never succeed. A *pure* tone will be obtained with a properly formed embouchure, but a *big* tone cannot be *formed*, it must be *blown*. Because air is the motivating power behind all brass playing, we must carefully consider the best ways to utilize it for our purpose.

Understandably, most of us do not give much thought to the normal breathing process, since it is a most natural, involuntary action from the moment of birth. Still, if we study the mechanics of normal breathing in even the most elementary manner, it will help us understand more clearly the similarities and, more important, the differences between normal breathing and the breathing process as used in brass playing.

Normal inhalation is based on the simple fact that "nature abhors a vacuum." The lungs are encased in the chest cavity, and when this cavity is expanded, air must rush in to fill the void. When the chest cavity is enlarged, the air pressure inside the lungs is reduced, and the outside air, with its fifteen pounds of pressure per square inch, literally pushes its way down the throat, in order to equalize the pressure. Therefore, all inhalation requires is the expansion of the chest cavity, and one of our natural laws will finish the process.

Humans have two fundamental ways of expanding this chest cavity: the diaphragm can contract downward, effectively *lowering* the *bottom* of this cavity, and the ribs can expand *outward* increasing the *diameter* of the cavity. Both processes are important and both are used simultaneously. However, let us examine them separately for clearer understanding.

The diaphragm is a large platter-shaped muscle extending horizontally all the way across the body in the region of the lower ribs and above the abdomen. Its shape in repose could be compared to a large, rounded salad-bowl, upside-down and placed in the body just below the lungs. In fact, the heart and lungs are the only major body organs *above* the diaphragm, the stomach, intestines and other organs being completely sealed off below them by this arching muscle. See Fig. 31.

Remembering that the major function of a muscle is to contract and shorten, we can readily understand that when the diaphragm contracts, this shortening action flattens out its normal dome-shape, effectively pulling it down. This results in an enlarged chest cavity--but note that the stomach and all organs in the body *below* the diaphragm are consequently compressed. Thus we see that the actual *work* of breathing is done on the *inhalation*. Not only is effort required to contract the large diaphragm muscle, but its very downward movement creates pressure against the organs below it. Incidently, this is one of the reasons that deep breathing is advocated by so many physicians as an aid to good health--because of its massaging effect and the

58

exercise which it contributes to all the internal organs.

Our other means of changing the size of the chest cavity is through the proper use of the rib cage. This cage, or thorax, is not the simple basket-shaped container we might thoughtlessly assume it to be. On the contrary, it is a most ingeniously designed mechanism. Consider that nature has solved the problem of giving a rigid bony structure the flexibility to expand and contract comfortably to a considerable degree and yet keep its inherent strength. Some of the flexibility comes from the fact that all of the ribs are attached to the backbone with cartilage, which has a degree of flexibility. In front, the upper ribs attach to the sternum, a flat, vertical bone running lengthwise in the upper front of the chest. These also are attached with joints of cartilage. The lower five pairs of ribs do not come all the way around to the front of the chest. In fact, each succeedingly lower pair falls farther short of completing the circle, although attached, nevertheless, by succeedingly longer and consequently more flexible extensions of cartilage. The bottom two sets of ribs do not even attach to the front of the chest by cartilage, but simply float, hence their name, *floating ribs*.

Perhaps the most ingenious part of this design

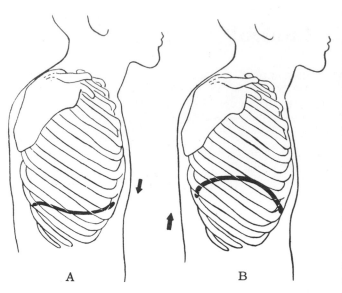

Fig. 31. Diagram of a person a) inhaling, b) exhaling. Arrow indicates the direction in which the diaphragm moves.

Reprinted with the permission of the publisher from SCIENCE BOOK OF THE HUMAN BODY by Edith E. Sproul. Published by Franklin Watts, Inc., New York.

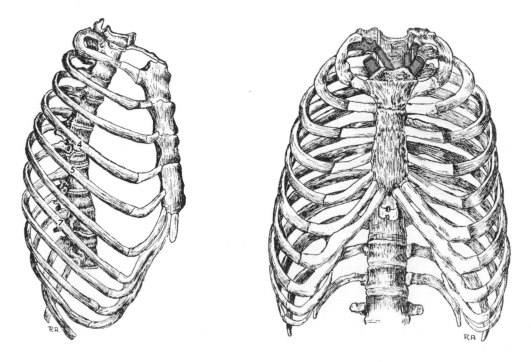

Fig. 32. Side view and front view of bones of the thorax.

Reprinted with the permission of the publisher from TEXTBOOK OF ANATOMY AND PHYSIOLOGY by Kimber, Gray, Stackpole and Leavell. 13th edition. Copyright 1955 by The Macmillan Company.

is the fact that the ribs do not travel around the chest from back to front in a horizontal manner like the hoops on a barrel. Look at Fig. 32 closely, and you will see that they not only attach at a lower point in front than in back in each case, but they also curve *down* from the spine to the sides and then back up again toward the front. This cage of "drooping" ribs is interlaced with muscles called *intercostals*. Upon inhalation the intercostal and several other muscles contract, pulling the sides of the drooping ribs upward. This in turn lifts the droop of the ribs in an outward as well as upward direction, the cartilage joints being amply flexible to permit this. Normal breathing activates these muscles in an almost involuntary manner, but just knowing the principal involved and being conscious of the role of the intercostal muscles will give us another voluntary control of our breathing process which will substantially increase our vital capacity.

In contrast to the effort needed for inhalation, mild though this effort is, *normal* exhalation requires no effort at all. Simply "let go", or relax, and all the contracted muscles return to their "in-repose" position. The diaphragm resumes its dome-shape, the intercostal muscles relax to allow the rib-cage to spring back to its smaller diameter, and the lower organs, relieved of the pressure exerted on them by the contracted diaphragm, now expand upward, helping the diaphragm assume its relaxed upward position.

Note that this is *normal* respiration. After a lifetime of this involuntary, effortless exhalation, it is no wonder that the average beginning brass student tries to play his instrument with this same weak, "pushless" air-stream. Once he realizes that the air-stream must not only fight its way past several points of resistance, but must also vibrate a brass instrument weighing several pounds with sufficient volume to be heard at the back of an auditorium, he will begin to understand the need for really *blowing* the instrument. He will realize that the projection of this air-column cannot be the same passive exhalation used in normal breathing, but must be something infinitely more steady and irresistable. Finally, he will feel the control and steadiness which come from a comfortably energetic "push" of air, and will get the same feel of "follow-through" with his air-column that a good golfer feels in his golf swing.

There is a certain spirit to correct blowing, as I have tried to indicate, and sometimes a bit of imagination helps to capture this spirit. The average player spends many hours a week practicing in some little, low-ceilinged, ten-foot square studio. No wonder he forgets to play in a full, expansive manner! I often shut my eyes while practicing in

such a room and imagine that I am playing a solo in a big auditorium such as Chicago's Orchestra Hall (the concert hall most closely associated with my own performances), accompanied by an orchestra comprising one hundred fine musicians, each producing a big, beautiful tone. Then the need for a projecting, resonant tone is most graphically realized, and, as a consequence, I play my instrument in a much more singing manner. It might seem much too loud in my little studio, but I realize that performing in the studio is not my ultimate goal and so continue to imagine my concert-hall surroundings and play accordingly. Just this simple bit of visualizing automatically improves my breathing, and consequently my tone, to a pronounced degree.

Inhalation

Certainly proper and copious *inhalation* must precede successful blowing. Obviously, if the player does not first inhale a generous quantity of air, he cannot, a moment later, project a large, sustained air-column. Childish as such an observation may seem, it is at this point in the breathing cycle that the student frequently fails. In my opinion, his shallow breathing is often due to his honest conviction that he is precisely emulating his teacher's inhalation. The teacher should be aware of this tendency and be ready to correct it. For the advanced player and teacher can become so efficient and apparently casual with his deep, silent, extremely rapid inhalation that the observer gets the distinct impression that only a shallow breath was taken. I occasionally demonstrate that such is not the case by playing a passage for the student during which I take a pre-arranged breath, to be followed by an extended passage during which I do not breathe. It is apparently one of these quick, shallow breaths, but a moment later, as I continue this extended, full-toned passage, it becomes obvious that this final breath must have been deceptively deep, or the following phrase would be a physical impossibility. Thus the first step in teaching correct deep breathing is to convince the student that such breaths are really necessary and that the teacher, in spite of appearances, does practice what he preaches. Once the student is firmly convinced that he must inhale as much air as he intends to exhale, he will be on his way toward successful breathing.

You remember that there are two main functions involved in inhalation: contracting the diaphragm downward, and expanding the rib-cage outward and upward. Deep, rapid breaths are obtained by employing *both* functions consciously and simultaneously. In order to fully develop and combine both types of inhalation, it is beneficial to practice each one separately, adding the other type only when the first has reached capacity. To do this: forcefully contract the diaphragm and lower it, at the same time keeping the ribs absolutely still (as though the chest were bound with iron bands); when the diaphragm is firmly pulled down and no more air can be inhaled through its use, expand the rib-cage outward and upward as far as possible, and notice how much additional air can be inhaled. This will demonstrate clearly that each function can do its share in bringing in more air. When this exercise can be done with each phase distinctly separated from the other, begin to blend them together, so that just as the diaphragm reaches bottom, the ribs start to expand. This will result in one long, leisurely inhalation.

Next, reverse the exercise, first expanding the rib-cage. Only after it is fully expanded, lower the diaphragm as far as possible. When these actions are clearly separated, blend them together so that the diaphragm begins to lower just as the rib-cage reaches its fullest expansion. As a result of practicing these two exercises, you will become acutely aware of the existence of *both* breathing functions and will start to control and combine them at will. Of course, the final application will consist of using them simultaneously, and this should comprise the third exercise of our group. Slowly lower the diaphragm and at the same time expand the rib-cage. Both actions should now be felt distinctly and yet be combined into one natural action. When this can be done smoothly and deeply, begin to practice this combined action to obtain the utmost possible rapidity, for it must be done rapidly in order to phrase music with the least possible interruption. As we increase the speed of this deep inhalation, the throat will start to impede the huge quantity of air that is suddenly sucked down into the lungs by the efficient use of this double-action breath. This results not only in slowing down the inhalation, but also in an all too audible wheeze or gasp. We must prevent this by opening the glottis (the space between the vocal cords) fully, and by keeping the tongue well down and out of the way. It is easy to fall into the bad habit of only partially opening the throat, which causes the inhalation to emit a hissing sound—a sort of *inhaled* whisper. But we have the ability to open the glottis wide so that the hiss does not take place. Instead, a deep-pitched, very quiet sigh results. This is the feeling we wish to develop in the throat during our deep, rapid inhalations—the feeling that the throat is as big and unrestricted as a length of stovepipe!

All the foregoing could perhaps be summed up by calling our brass playing inhalation a sort of huge, silent, rapid gasp—the kind of gasp caused by the reaction of stepping suddenly into an ice-cold shower on a hot day.

Exhalation

Only after having considered the means of inhaling large quantities of air rapidly and silently are we really properly prepared to consider how to emit, or better, *project* this air through the instrument. For the air cannot be permitted to leisurely *drift into* the horn as in normal exhalation, but must be steadily *projected through* the instrument, although at times this projection is very mild.

This steadiness is achieved to a great degree by the steady contraction of the muscles around the waist, in the region of the abdomen. During *normal* exhalation, the suddenly relaxed diaphragm tends to spring upward to its domed, in-repose position, in a rather uncontrolled and unpredictable manner. In fact, its speed is almost entirely controlled by how wide the throat is opened. This sort of control, or lack of it, is completely unsuitable for musical purposes. But, when we begin to contract the waist muscles, putting even more pressure on the lower organs (which you remember, already have some pressure placed on them from the lowered diaphragm), we *consciously* put into use nature's perfect design, in which every set of muscles must have an antagonistic or opposing set to furnish movement in the opposite direction. Instead of permitting the diaphragm to *relax* back into its reposed position, which is a negative action at best, we actively contract its antagonistic muscles, which are the muscles around the waist. For when this complex set of waist muscles is contracted, the organs below the diaphragm must be pushed somewhere, and that somewhere is *up!* Now, instead of being at the mercy of the relaxed and *passively* rising diaphragm, we are *actively contracting* muscles for positive control of the speed and energy with which the diaphragm is *pushed* upward.

At the same time that this action takes place, the muscles across the *front* of the chest contract, pulling the rib-cage in toward its smaller diameter. Earlier, during the inhalation, the *opposing muscles* at the *back* of the chest contracted, expanding the rib-cage. However, this expansion and contraction of the rib-cage takes place so normally and automatically that I have never felt the need of stressing it beyond the few *inhaling* exercises suggested earlier. The real need is the steady upward push under the diaphragm, which is furnished by the waist muscles contracting around the internal organs below the diaphragm.

Some students might feel a little squeamish about the idea of the internal organs being pushed around a bit by this contraction, but competent physicians have assured me that this internal massage and exercise is most beneficial and should be considered an added bonus to the other satisfactions derived from brass playing.

Exhalation Resistance

Resistance is another important consideration in gaining steadiness of breath exhalation. As an illustration, resistance is what gives *steadiness* to the hissing sound of a "slow-leak" in an automobile tire; tire "blow-out" is the result of all resistance giving way. While I do not advocate the production of a brass instrument tone which sounds like a "slow-leak", this is certainly closer to what we want than a "blow-out"! For in playing a brass instrument, we need to spin out a long stream of air, and this can only be accomplished through resistance somewhere along the path of the air. We have all heard the admonition to "inhale a ball and exhale a thread". This is a very apt description, but, in my opinion, it is not quite graphic nor emphatic enough. I would change it to, "for big passages, inhale a basket-ball and exhale a rope; for soft passages, inhale a tennis-ball and exhale a thread". Regardless of how we phrase it, the fact remains that we inhale as quickly as possible through a wide-open, unresisting throat and exhale against certain optional or unavoidable points of resistance. When we exhale through the instrument, we need this resistance to extend the stream of air for as long a time as necessary. Of course, as we play louder, we use a bigger stream and consequently use less resistance. This, in turn, results in shorter sustaining ability.

Perhaps before considering the various points of resistance, this is a good time to warn of a bad habit prevalent among wind players which is particularly detrimental to their soft playing and which again points up the need for resistance somewhere. The general pressure of abdomen and intercostal muscles can be made very light, resulting in an exhalation of little "push". In my opinion, this principle of using very little pressure from the diaphragm for the production of soft volume is a serious error. All of us will instinctively support a long loud note quite correctly, the very act of sustaining such a note requiring proper procedure. When I can get a pupil to play with a big, sustained tone, I feel that he has automatically called into use the proper breathing muscles. The real danger of blowing a brass instrument incorrectly occurs during soft passages. At such times, the player has the choice of simply pushing very lightly with the diaphragm and letting the air *drift* through an open,

unresisting passage, or of pushing *quite firmly* with the diaphragm, but *holding back* this stronger air-column to the desired volume by *resisting* the air somewhere. I do not believe that a large, strong muscle like the diaphragm has enough finesse to *float* a very soft *pianissimo* through the instrument with a great degree of steadiness. On the other hand, the moderately heavy push which I advocate (not as forceful as would be required for *forte*, but perhaps a push capable of producing a light *mezzo-forte*) can be converted to an extremely steady *pianissimo* by holding it back with resistance. Here again we have the idea of the "slow-leak" which is the result of steady, firm pressure through a small hole.

Here is another analogy which might clarify this concept. If one wished to trickle a tiny stream of cold water into his too-hot cup of coffee, he could phone the pumping station and request it to slow down the pumps, and then proceed to turn the faucet on full force. This would possibly result in the desired trickle. But, with the pumps slowed down or stopped, the trickle would be anything but steady. However, the thing that amuses us with this idea is the incongruity of doing a simple act "the hard way". How much easier and simpler to let the pumps go ahead in their efficient way and simply "crack-open" the faucet a tiny bit, until the desired trickle appears. Not only is it easier and faster, but the trickle has an entirely different character. It does not dribble, flood and drip by turns, but forms a little rod of water, round, firm and steady. Even its diameter is completely controllable.

In just this same way, the steady diaphragm pressure against a "cracked-open" air-column lets through a firm, steady rod of air of any diameter desired. When this concept becomes part of one's playing procedure, *pianissimo* will hold no terrors. The diaphragm and other muscles can act firmly and purposefully, and yet the held back air-stream is tiny and marvelously *steady*, resulting in a *pianissimo* which is actually a physical pleasure to play. All the preceding, then, is an admonition not to eliminate resistance and substitute a pushless air-stream in order to obtain soft tones.

Where and how is this resistance obtained? It can occur at several places. Some of these are desirable, and some are detrimental to artistic playing; some are optional and completely adjustable, and others are unavoidable and not adjustable. Let me enumerate these points of resistance, good and bad, in the order in which they occur as the air travels from the lungs.

1.) The first point of resistance is found in the throat, at a point called the *glottis*. See Fig. 33.

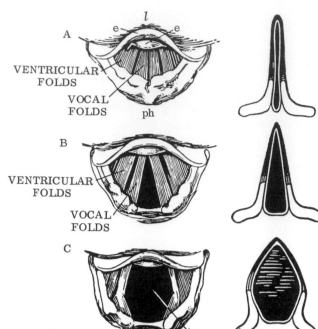

A

VENTRICULAR FOLDS

VOCAL FOLDS

B

VENTRICULAR FOLDS

VOCAL FOLDS

C

Fig. 33. The larynx as seen by means of the laryngo-scope in different conditions of the glottis. A, while singing a high note; B, in quiet breathing; C, during a deep inspiration; l, base of tongue; e, upper free edge of epiglottis; e', cushion of epiglottis; ph, part of anterior wall of pharynx; tr, trachea.

Reprinted with the permission of the publisher from TEXTBOOK OF ANATOMY AND PHYSIOLOGY, by Kimber, Gray, Stackpole and Leavell. 13th edition. Copyright 1955 by The Macmillan Company.

The glottis, being the *opening* between the vocal cords, is not a tangible thing, but simply the space between these cords which is completely adjustable in size from wide-open to absolutely shut. Furthermore, although it is involved in the important adjustments used to vary the pitch and quality of the voice in singing, it is used quite naturally and correctly in everyday living to furnish resistance for many purposes, at which times the vocal cords *do not sound*. For instance, the glottis is completely closed during an act such as lifting a heavy weight. It is exploded open during a cough, or when clearing the throat. It is partially open for whispering, and wide-open for a rapid exhalation such as one would use for a "panting" effect. In this way, the glottis is used as a natural valve, and not for the purpose of vocalizing. I mention the fact that this is a perfectly natural, everyday function of the glottis, because many brass players react in horror when I suggest using this valve for purposes of playing our instruments. They evidently feel that I am advocating the use of a "tight throat", a condition

all teachers have carefully avoided from the inception of brass playing. To me, the bad habit of playing with a "tight throat" means the forcible tightening of the neck muscles, or worse yet, the *sounding* of the vocal cords, resulting in a low moaning or groaning noise, heard while the instrument is played, and I have fought these bad habits just as diligently as any other brass teacher. The proper use of the glottis is natural and effective and is quite likely being used by most successful brass players, either consciously or subconsciously.

To experience this glottis action, simply whisper a long held "oh", loud enough to be heard ten or fifteen feet away. If the glottis were kept wide-open instead of partially closed, the "oh" would remain quite silent, and the air, with an equal amount of diaphragm pressure, would burst out in a big, silent ball--our inhaled "basket-ball" in reverse!

Two simple exercises can be practiced which will develop conscious control of the glottis. Since the glottis is in constant use in everyday activity, these exercises are not designed to strengthen it, but only to make the player more fully conscious of its existence and function.

First, after a deep inhalation, start exhaling slowly through a wide-open throat. Then, very gradually start to close the "whisper valve"--the glottis--creating more and more resistance until the valve is completely shut. Be careful not to activate the vocal cords, which could mistakenly be brought into play in an attempt to furnish the needed resistance. When this gradual shutting of the valve can be controlled steadily, try varying the speed with which it is done. Finally, use this process while holding a long tone on the instrument, starting with a proper attack and a nice, full volume. The *diminuendo* obtained by this gradual "valving-shut" of the air quantity should be much superior to the *diminuendo* obtained by gradually weakening the *diaphragm push* while keeping the glottis wide-open. Of course, one does not continue to push the diaphragm violently while making a *diminuendo*, but should continue a *comfortable* push at all volumes, and this push, in conjunction with the glottis, will give a steadiness, not attainable in any other way, to the tone at any volume.

The second exercise, being the practice of a *crescendo*, is the reverse of the first. Start the exhalation against the resistance of the completely closed glottis. Again, do not use an absurd amount of pressure, but simply a comfortable *mezzoforte* push. Carefully "crack-open" the glottis, and then gradually open it wider, at the same time increasing the diaphragm push, consistent with the air quantities needed for the *crescendo*. Try this exercise at varying speeds. Then finally apply it to the instrument for a controlled *crescendo*. It should result in a *crescendo* of great steadiness and without the "bulges" so noticeable when the diaphragm alone tries to make the *crescendo* through a wide-open throat. Most players use this glottis valve in a natural manner, and these exercises are helpful in reminding them of its function. But the exercises will be of inestimable value to those players who have never experienced the control that it will contribute to their playing.

2.) The second point of resistance is optional and adjustable and is located at the back of the tongue. By arching the back of the tongue high up toward the roof of the mouth as though pronouncing "ee" in the word "key", we can feel this resistance take place. At first appraisal, this method of furnishing resistance might seem as flexible and natural as the glottis control, having equally infinite adjustment and an easy voluntary movement. However, when we recall that it is this same arching or lowering of the tongue which we use for the "ah-ee" or "ee-ah" effect so helpful in upward or downward slurs, we realize that there could be a serious conflict in this action of the tongue in many musical passages. For instance, what would the poor, confused tongue do on an upward slur which required a *crescendo*? The *crescendo*, if the tongue is to furnish the "resistance variation", requires the tongue to make the transition from "ee" to "ah", but the upward slur requires the articulation "ah-ee"! The two conflicting actions literally cancel out each other, and we gain neither the lift to the upward slur, nor the enlarging air-column so necessary to the *crescendo*. Thus it seems simpler and more logical to assign the resistance adjustment to the glottis and reserve the tongue-base action for its function in the mechanics of slurring. (Perhaps this "ah" or "ee" use of the tongue could be more aptly defined as an "altitude regulator", because it is used in changing altitude, slurs being one phase of "altitude changing".) The arching of the tongue lends itself so naturally to slurring, or changing from one range to another, that it would seem detrimental to assign it the task of also regulating the air-resistance—or volume. Nor is this action, in my opinion and that of many of my esteemed colleagues, quite so natural or voluntary as the use of the glottis as a "volume control".

3.) The third point of resistance met by the air-column is the tip of the tongue. As its resistance is total before an attack and should be nil after the attack, it is obvious that this is not the type of resistance we are considering in this discussion. I mention it only to be thorough (and perhaps to prevent criticism—"You forgot to mention the tip of the tongue!").

4.) The fourth point of resistance to the air-column is, of course, the lip-aperture. The resistance here *can* be optional and adjustable. However, surely it is better to think of it as optional, but *not* adjustable. For to adjust this critical opening with the thought of obtaining some desired amount of air-column resistance would be to ignore the fact that this opening has just about all it can do to form itself into the right size and shape to create the correct pitch at all volumes and with desirable tone quality. To require it to form a size and shape to satisfy a need for any particular resistance would be most detrimental. So it must *not* adjust for this purpose. However, I think of the lip-aperture resistance as *optional* because all of us at some time in our playing lives adopt an individual manner of playing which creates more or less resistance in this lip-aperture. After years of practice, this resistance, be it little or great, becomes chronic, and the player learns to live with it. Usually, the inferior player adopts a too tight lip-aperture. But fortunately, it is in this feature that adjustment is *optional*. Any tight, tense brass player can learn to play with the jaw held down, the lips a bit more parted, and the embouchure muscles definitely more relaxed. In this choice we have an option. But once the player has chosen to let the air flow past the lips with a minimum of resistance, he is not likely ever again to want to feel the lips furnishing resistance for the sake of resistance. When this free, relaxed option is chosen, it becomes almost a way of life, and its advocate would never think of his lips as being *adjustable* for the purpose of creating more resistance. So use the lips for their proper purpose—the formation of relaxed, clear notes of definite pitch—and relegate the air-column resistance to another more suitable spot.

5.) The air-column next encounters resistance as it enters the small hole at the end of the mouthpiece cup—the "bore" of the mouthpiece. The size of this mouthpiece bore is obviously *optional*, but once a mouthpiece is chosen and used regularly, it could certainly not be considered *adjustable*. So although we have the option of choosing the most personally desirable mouthpiece, once we have it, we must play on it with no regard for how it might affect the air-column resistance. Even though it is a most important tool for obtaining any desired amount of *permanent* resistance, we cannot consider the mouthpiece a likely place to find voluntary and immediate adjustment of air-column resistance.

6.) The last point of resistance is the instrument itself. In any type of brass instrument there are the choices of weight, thickness of metal, various alloys, diameter of tubing, and design itself. All these things determine the playing resistance of the instrument. Of course, each player, after trying several makes, knows instinctively which one he wants to play. Once he owns and plays a certain instrument, its built-in resistance is there to stay and thus is not adjustable.

In summary, of the six points of resistance we have considered, only one has complete flexibility from fully opened to fully closed, a natural, voluntary means of obtaining this flexibility, and no other conflicting duties to perform. That point is the glottis, mentioned as number one of our resistance points. For this reason, the control of the glottis has been thoroughly discussed, and I sincerely believe that anyone who studies and practices the ideas put forth on that subject can make himself a better brass player.

There is a tendency among wind instrumentalists and singers to approach the problems of breathing with an awed timidity—as if these were so eso-teric or mysterious that only the favored few could ever hope to solve the various intricacies. We hear all kinds of instructions, each of which claims to unlock the secret of correct breathing—"push against the belt buckle", "turn the diaphragm inside-out", "feel a piston coming up from the stomach", "let the ribs float out from the body", "blow out a candle from ten feet away", "project", "spin the tone". Any one of these expressions might help some individual, but in the long run, I think they frighten more students than they help.

Without a doubt, correct use of the breath is an exceedingly important part of playing a brass instrument. But for all its importance, we must remember that this type of breathing is closely associated with the breathing we have done from the moment of birth, and perhaps this realization will take some of the fear and mysticism out of the relatively simple act of "blowing a horn".

9. Conclusion

The great number of foregoing pages might lead you to believe that brass playing is extremely difficult--or at least lead you to believe that *I* think it is! Such is not the case. I believe brass playing is quite natural an act--an almost instinctive one--else why do we find various types of horns being played by man down through antiquity? And how would the first players, having no teachers, develop their skill if the act were not more or less instinctive? Some of them must have played quite well in this primitive, but intuitive manner, or the art would not have been perpetuated, as any modern would-be brass player who is suffering because of wrong procedures can tell you. This thought--that brass playing can and should be a natural, instinctive act--is very helpful when one gets "off the track" occasionally. And all brass players do! At such a time, it is wise to "coast", look for the more obvious troubles, and nurture that instinct, that intuition, back to its rightful and important place.

This book is long because there are many problems to cover, but luckily no one player has them all! So, although solving all the problems discussed herein would be an almost insurmountable task for anyone, most of you will read through the book and intelligently say to yourself, "*This* problem and its solution certainly pertains to me; however, that one does not apply to me at all." I sincerely hope that each of you can say that you needed only a very few pages of this book. This is as it should be. The would-be brass player who needed correction on every phase of playing discussed here would be so sadly lacking in this brass playing instinct that he should perhaps drop the entire project in favor of a different career.

When one has this instinct for brass playing, he needs but two other attributes to make his playing successful--moderately normal teeth, lips and general physique, and a feeling for music, so that when the physical control is gained, that which comes out of the horn-bell is worth hearing. Did I say two attributes? There is that third one—willingness to practice! Without this one, all the others are completely worthless. But, having these attributes, make use of them, and the final result will profoundly enhance and enrich your life.

When this ability is put to use professionally, it can lead to an interesting, satisfying and remunerative career—one which amply pays back the effort invested. But perhaps the *amateur*, with his ability to laugh-off the occasional broken note, enjoys brass playing the most, as he can collaborate with friends, express himself artistically, and indulge in his hobby, all at the same time. The professional, of course, gets all these pleasures, too, save the one of laughing at his broken notes. On the other hand, he gets paid for his music, which at times almost makes up for the loss of this other privilege.

Therefore, pursue your brass playing with enthusiasm, and let the results take you where they will. This much I can guarantee: Mastering your horn will repay your efforts many times over, and this inanimate brass object will then take on an entity and personality, which like any other true friend, can enrich and vitalize your entire life.

End.

The following pages can be used to personalize and enhance the value of this book. Use them for your own notes, comments, reference to pages important to you, and above all, as a scrapbook in which you can, from time to time, paste photographs and clippings of the finest brass artists in the act of performing on their instruments.